Business Math Handbook

to accompany

Practical Business Math Procedures

Eleventh Edition

Jeffrey Slater
North Shore Community College
Danvers, Massachusetts

Sharon M. Wittry
Pikes Peak Community College
Colorado Springs, Colorado

McGraw-Hill Irwin

Business Math Handbook to accompany
PRACTICAL BUSINESS MATH PROCEDURES, ELEVENTH EDITION
Jeffrey Slater and Sharon M. Wittry

Published by McGraw-Hill/Irwin, an imprint of The McGraw-Hill Companies, Inc., 1221 Avenue of the Americas, New York, NY 10020. Copyright © 2014, 2011, 2008 by The McGraw-Hill Companies, Inc. All rights reserved. Printed in the United States of America.

7 8 9 0 ROV/ROV 1 0 9 8 7 6 5

ISBN 978-0-07-753380-9
MHID 0-07-753380-1

www.mhhe.com

PERIOD	TABLE 12-1 COMPOUND VALUE OF $1	TABLE 12-3 PRESENT VALUE OF $1	TABLE 13-1 AMOUNT OF ANNUITY OF $1	TABLE 13-2 PRESENT VALUE OF ANNUITY OF $1	TABLE 13-3 SINKING FUND VALUE OF $1
1	1.0050	0.9950	1.0000	0.9950	1.0000
2	1.0100	0.9901	2.0050	1.9851	0.4988
3	1.0151	0.9851	3.0150	2.9702	0.3317
4	1.0202	0.9802	4.0301	3.9505	0.2481
5	1.0253	0.9754	5.0503	4.9259	0.1980
6	1.0304	0.9705	6.0755	5.8964	0.1646
7	1.0355	0.9657	7.1059	6.8621	0.1407
8	1.0407	0.9609	8.1414	7.8230	0.1228
9	1.0459	0.9561	9.1821	8.7791	0.1089
10	1.0511	0.9513	10.2280	9.7304	0.0978
11	1.0564	0.9466	11.2792	10.6770	0.0887
12	1.0617	0.9419	12.3356	11.6189	0.0811
13	1.0670	0.9372	13.3973	12.5562	0.0746
14	1.0723	0.9326	14.4643	13.4887	0.0691
15	1.0777	0.9279	15.5365	14.4166	0.0644
16	1.0831	0.9233	16.6142	15.3399	0.0602
17	1.0885	0.9187	17.6973	16.2586	0.0565
18	1.0939	0.9141	18.7858	17.1728	0.0532
19	1.0994	0.9096	19.8797	18.0824	0.0503
20	1.1049	0.9051	20.9791	18.9874	0.0477
21	1.1104	0.9006	22.0840	19.8880	0.0453
22	1.1160	0.8961	23.1945	20.7841	0.0431
23	1.1216	0.8916	24.3104	21.6757	0.0411
24	1.1272	0.8872	25.4320	22.5629	0.0393
25	1.1328	0.8828	26.5591	23.4457	0.0377
26	1.1385	0.8784	27.6919	24.3240	0.0361
27	1.1442	0.8740	28.8304	25.1980	0.0347
28	1.1499	0.8697	29.9746	26.0677	0.0334
29	1.1556	0.8653	31.1245	26.9331	0.0321
30	1.1614	0.8610	32.2801	27.7941	0.0310
31	1.1672	0.8567	33.4414	28.6508	0.0299
32	1.1730	0.8525	34.6087	29.5033	0.0289
33	1.1789	0.8482	35.7817	30.3515	0.0279
34	1.1848	0.8440	36.9606	31.1956	0.0271
35	1.1907	0.8398	38.1454	32.0354	0.0262
36	1.1967	0.8356	39.3361	32.8710	0.0254
37	1.2027	0.8315	40.5328	33.7025	0.0247
38	1.2087	0.8274	41.7355	34.5299	0.0240
39	1.2147	0.8232	42.9441	35.3531	0.0233
40	1.2208	0.8191	44.1589	36.1723	0.0226
41	1.2269	0.8151	45.3797	36.9873	0.0220
42	1.2330	0.8110	46.6066	37.7983	0.0215
43	1.2392	0.8070	47.8396	38.6053	0.0209
44	1.2454	0.8030	49.0788	39.4083	0.0204
45	1.2516	0.7990	50.3242	40.2072	0.0199
46	1.2579	0.7950	51.5759	41.0022	0.0194
47	1.2642	0.7910	52.8337	41.7932	0.0189
48	1.2705	0.7871	54.0979	42.5804	0.0185
49	1.2768	0.7832	55.3684	43.3635	0.0181
50	1.2832	0.7793	56.6452	44.1428	0.0177

1%

PERIOD	TABLE 12-1 COMPOUND VALUE OF $1	TABLE 12-3 PRESENT VALUE OF $1	TABLE 13-1 AMOUNT OF ANNUITY OF $1	TABLE 13-2 PRESENT VALUE OF ANNUITY OF $1	TABLE 13-3 SINKING FUND VALUE OF $1
1	1.0100	0.9901	1.0000	0.9901	1.0000
2	1.0201	0.9803	2.0100	1.9704	0.4975
3	1.0303	0.9706	3.0301	2.9410	0.3300
4	1.0406	0.9610	4.0604	3.9020	0.2463
5	1.0510	0.9515	5.1010	4.8534	0.1960
6	1.0615	0.9420	6.1520	5.7955	0.1625
7	1.0721	0.9327	7.2135	6.7282	0.1386
8	1.0829	0.9235	8.2857	7.6517	0.1207
9	1.0937	0.9143	9.3685	8.5660	0.1067
10	1.1046	0.9053	10.4622	9.4713	0.0956
11	1.1157	0.8963	11.5668	10.3676	0.0865
12	1.1268	0.8874	12.6825	11.2551	0.0788
13	1.1381	0.8787	13.8093	12.1337	0.0724
14	1.1495	0.8700	14.9474	13.0037	0.0669
15	1.1610	0.8613	16.0969	13.8650	0.0621
16	1.1726	0.8528	17.2579	14.7179	0.0579
17	1.1843	0.8444	18.4304	15.5622	0.0543
18	1.1961	0.8360	19.6147	16.3983	0.0510
19	1.2081	0.8277	20.8109	17.2260	0.0481
20	1.2202	0.8195	22.0190	18.0455	0.0454
21	1.2324	0.8114	23.2392	18.8570	0.0430
22	1.2447	0.8034	24.4716	19.6604	0.0409
23	1.2572	0.7954	25.7163	20.4558	0.0389
24	1.2697	0.7876	26.9735	21.2434	0.0371
25	1.2824	0.7798	28.2432	22.0231	0.0354
26	1.2953	0.7720	29.5256	22.7952	0.0339
27	1.3082	0.7644	30.8209	23.5596	0.0324
28	1.3213	0.7568	32.1291	24.3164	0.0311
29	1.3345	0.7493	33.4504	25.0658	0.0299
30	1.3478	0.7419	34.7849	25.8077	0.0287
31	1.3613	0.7346	36.1327	26.5423	0.0277
32	1.3749	0.7273	37.4941	27.2696	0.0267
33	1.3887	0.7201	38.8690	27.9897	0.0257
34	1.4026	0.7130	40.2577	28.7027	0.0248
35	1.4166	0.7059	41.6603	29.4086	0.0240
36	1.4308	0.6989	43.0769	30.1075	0.0232
37	1.4451	0.6920	44.5076	30.7995	0.0225
38	1.4595	0.6852	45.9527	31.4847	0.0218
39	1.4741	0.6784	47.4122	32.1630	0.0211
40	1.4889	0.6717	48.8864	32.8347	0.0205
41	1.5038	0.6650	50.3752	33.4997	0.0199
42	1.5188	0.6584	51.8790	34.1581	0.0193
43	1.5340	0.6519	53.3978	34.8100	0.0187
44	1.5493	0.6454	54.9317	35.4554	0.0182
45	1.5648	0.6391	56.4811	36.0945	0.0177
46	1.5805	0.6327	58.0459	36.7272	0.0172
47	1.5963	0.6265	59.6263	37.3537	0.0168
48	1.6122	0.6203	61.2226	37.9739	0.0163
49	1.6283	0.6141	62.8348	38.5881	0.0159
50	1.6446	0.6080	64.4632	39.1961	0.0155

PERIOD	TABLE 12-1 COMPOUND VALUE OF $1	TABLE 12-3 PRESENT VALUE OF $1	TABLE 13-1 AMOUNT OF ANNUITY OF $1	TABLE 13-2 PRESENT VALUE OF ANNUITY OF $1	TABLE 13-3 SINKING FUND VALUE OF $1
1	1.0150	0.9852	1.0000	0.9852	1.0000
2	1.0302	0.9707	2.0150	1.9559	0.4963
3	1.0457	0.9563	3.0452	2.9122	0.3284
4	1.0614	0.9422	4.0909	3.8544	0.2444
5	1.0773	0.9283	5.1522	4.7826	0.1941
6	1.0934	0.9145	6.2295	5.6972	0.1605
7	1.1098	0.9010	7.3230	6.5982	0.1366
8	1.1265	0.8877	8.4328	7.4859	0.1186
9	1.1434	0.8746	9.5593	8.3605	0.1046
10	1.1605	0.8617	10.7027	9.2222	0.0934
11	1.1780	0.8489	11.8632	10.0711	0.0843
12	1.1960	0.8364	13.0412	10.9075	0.0767
13	1.2135	0.8240	14.2368	11.7315	0.0702
14	1.2318	0.8119	15.4503	12.5433	0.0647
15	1.2502	0.7999	16.6821	13.3432	0.0599
16	1.2690	0.7880	17.9323	14.1312	0.0558
17	1.2880	0.7764	19.2013	14.9076	0.0521
18	1.3073	0.7649	20.4893	15.6725	0.0488
19	1.3270	0.7536	21.7966	16.4261	0.0459
20	1.3469	0.7425	23.1236	17.1686	0.0432
21	1.3671	0.7315	24.4704	17.9001	0.0409
22	1.3876	0.7207	25.8375	18.6208	0.0387
23	1.4084	0.7100	27.2250	19.3308	0.0367
24	1.4295	0.6995	28.6334	20.0304	0.0349
25	1.4510	0.6892	30.0629	20.7196	0.0333
26	1.4727	0.6790	31.5138	21.3986	0.0317
27	1.4948	0.6690	32.9866	22.0676	0.0303
28	1.5172	0.6591	34.4813	22.7267	0.0290
29	1.5400	0.6494	35.9986	23.3760	0.0278
30	1.5631	0.6398	37.5385	24.0158	0.0266
31	1.5865	0.6303	39.1016	24.6461	0.0256
32	1.6103	0.6210	40.6881	25.2671	0.0246
33	1.6345	0.6118	42.2984	25.8789	0.0236
34	1.6590	0.6028	43.9329	26.4817	0.0228
35	1.6839	0.5939	45.5919	27.0755	0.0219
36	1.7091	0.5851	47.2758	27.6606	0.0212
37	1.7348	0.5764	48.9849	28.2371	0.0204
38	1.7608	0.5679	50.7197	28.8050	0.0197
39	1.7872	0.5595	52.4805	29.3645	0.0191
40	1.8140	0.5513	54.2677	29.9158	0.0184
41	1.8412	0.5431	56.0817	30.4589	0.0178
42	1.8688	0.5351	57.9229	30.9940	0.0173
43	1.8969	0.5272	59.7917	31.5212	0.0167
44	1.9253	0.5194	61.6886	32.0405	0.0162
45	1.9542	0.5117	63.6139	32.5523	0.0157
46	1.9835	0.5042	65.5681	33.0564	0.0153
47	2.0133	0.4967	67.5516	33.5531	0.0148
48	2.0435	0.4894	69.5649	34.0425	0.0144
49	2.0741	0.4821	71.6084	34.5246	0.0140
50	2.1052	0.4750	73.6825	34.9996	0.0136

2%

PERIOD	TABLE 12-1 COMPOUND VALUE OF $1	TABLE 12-3 PRESENT VALUE OF $1	TABLE 13-1 AMOUNT OF ANNUITY OF $1	TABLE 13-2 PRESENT VALUE OF ANNUITY OF $1	TABLE 13-3 SINKING FUND VALUE OF $1
1	1.0200	0.9804	1.0000	0.9804	1.0000
2	1.0404	0.9612	2.0200	1.9416	0.4951
3	1.0612	0.9423	3.0604	2.8839	0.3268
4	1.0824	0.9238	4.1216	3.8077	0.2426
5	1.1041	0.9057	5.2040	4.7134	0.1922
6	1.1262	0.8880	6.3081	5.6014	0.1585
7	1.1487	0.8706	7.4343	6.4720	0.1345
8	1.1717	0.8535	8.5829	7.3255	0.1165
9	1.1951	0.8368	9.7546	8.1622	0.1025
10	1.2190	0.8203	10.9497	8.9826	0.0913
11	1.2434	0.8043	12.1687	9.7868	0.0822
12	1.2682	0.7885	13.4120	10.5753	0.0746
13	1.2936	0.7730	14.6803	11.3483	0.0681
14	1.3195	0.7579	15.9739	12.1062	0.0626
15	1.3459	0.7430	17.2934	12.8492	0.0578
16	1.3728	0.7284	18.6392	13.5777	0.0537
17	1.4002	0.7142	20.0120	14.2918	0.0500
18	1.4282	0.7002	21.4122	14.9920	0.0467
19	1.4568	0.6864	22.8405	15.6784	0.0438
20	1.4859	0.6730	24.2973	16.3514	0.0412
21	1.5157	0.6598	25.7832	17.0112	0.0388
22	1.5460	0.6468	27.2989	17.6580	0.0366
23	1.5769	0.6342	28.8449	18.2922	0.0347
24	1.6084	0.6217	30.4218	18.9139	0.0329
25	1.6406	0.6095	32.0302	19.5234	0.0312
26	1.6734	0.5976	33.6708	20.1210	0.0297
27	1.7069	0.5859	35.3442	20.7069	0.0283
28	1.7410	0.5744	37.0511	21.2812	0.0270
29	1.7758	0.5631	38.7921	21.8443	0.0258
30	1.8114	0.5521	40.5679	22.3964	0.0247
31	1.8476	0.5412	42.3793	22.9377	0.0236
32	1.8845	0.5306	44.2269	23.4683	0.0226
33	1.9222	0.5202	46.1114	23.9885	0.0217
34	1.9607	0.5100	48.0336	24.4985	0.0208
35	1.9999	0.5000	49.9943	24.9986	0.0200
36	2.0399	0.4902	51.9942	25.4888	0.0192
37	2.0807	0.4806	54.0340	25.9694	0.0185
38	2.1223	0.4712	56.1147	26.4406	0.0178
39	2.1647	0.4619	58.2370	26.9025	0.0172
40	2.2080	0.4529	60.4017	27.3554	0.0166
41	2.2522	0.4440	62.6098	27.7994	0.0160
42	2.2972	0.4353	64.8620	28.2347	0.0154
43	2.3432	0.4268	67.1592	28.6615	0.0149
44	2.3900	0.4184	69.5024	29.0799	0.0144
45	2.4378	0.4102	71.8924	29.4901	0.0139
46	2.4866	0.4022	74.3302	29.8923	0.0135
47	2.5363	0.3943	76.8168	30.2865	0.0130
48	2.5871	0.3865	79.3532	30.6731	0.0126
49	2.6388	0.3790	81.9402	31.0520	0.0122
50	2.6916	0.3715	84.5790	31.4236	0.0118

2½%

PERIOD	TABLE 12-1 COMPOUND VALUE OF $1	TABLE 12-3 PRESENT VALUE OF $1	TABLE 13-1 AMOUNT OF ANNUITY OF $1	TABLE 13-2 PRESENT VALUE OF ANNUITY OF $1	TABLE 13-3 SINKING FUND VALUE OF $1
1	1.0250	0.9756	1.0000	0.9756	1.0000
2	1.0506	0.9518	2.0250	1.9274	0.4938
3	1.0769	0.9286	3.0756	2.8560	0.3251
4	1.1038	0.9060	4.1525	3.7620	0.2408
5	1.1314	0.8839	5.2563	4.6458	0.1902
6	1.1597	0.8623	6.3877	5.5081	0.1566
7	1.1887	0.8413	7.5474	6.3494	0.1325
8	1.2184	0.8207	8.7361	7.1701	0.1145
9	1.2489	0.8007	9.9545	7.9709	0.1005
10	1.2801	0.7812	11.2034	8.7521	0.0893
11	1.3121	0.7621	12.4835	9.5142	0.0801
12	1.3449	0.7436	13.7955	10.2578	0.0725
13	1.3785	0.7254	15.1404	10.9832	0.0660
14	1.4130	0.7077	16.5189	11.6909	0.0605
15	1.4483	0.6905	17.9319	12.3814	0.0558
16	1.4845	0.6736	19.3802	13.0550	0.0516
17	1.5216	0.6572	20.8647	13.7122	0.0479
18	1.5597	0.6412	22.3863	14.3534	0.0447
19	1.5986	0.6255	23.9460	14.9789	0.0418
20	1.6386	0.6103	25.5446	15.5892	0.0391
21	1.6796	0.5954	27.1832	16.1845	0.0368
22	1.7216	0.5809	28.8628	16.7654	0.0346
23	1.7646	0.5667	30.5844	17.3321	0.0327
24	1.8087	0.5529	32.3490	17.8850	0.0309
25	1.8539	0.5394	34.1577	18.4244	0.0293
26	1.9003	0.5262	36.0117	18.9506	0.0278
27	1.9478	0.5134	37.9120	19.4640	0.0264
28	1.9965	0.5009	39.8598	19.9649	0.0251
29	2.0464	0.4887	41.8563	20.4535	0.0239
30	2.0976	0.4767	43.9027	20.9303	0.0228
31	2.1500	0.4651	46.0002	21.3954	0.0217
32	2.2038	0.4538	48.1502	21.8492	0.0208
33	2.2588	0.4427	50.3540	22.2919	0.0199
34	2.3153	0.4319	52.6128	22.7238	0.0190
35	2.3732	0.4214	54.9282	23.1451	0.0182
36	2.4325	0.4111	57.3014	23.5562	0.0175
37	2.4933	0.4011	59.7339	23.9573	0.0167
38	2.5557	0.3913	62.2272	24.3486	0.0161
39	2.6196	0.3817	64.7829	24.7303	0.0154
40	2.6851	0.3724	67.4025	25.1028	0.0148
41	2.7522	0.3633	70.0875	25.4661	0.0143
42	2.8210	0.3545	72.8397	25.8206	0.0137
43	2.8915	0.3458	75.6607	26.1664	0.0132
44	2.9638	0.3374	78.5522	26.5038	0.0127
45	3.0379	0.3292	81.5160	26.8330	0.0123
46	3.1138	0.3211	84.5539	27.1542	0.0118
47	3.1917	0.3133	87.6678	27.4675	0.0114
48	3.2715	0.3057	90.8595	27.7731	0.0110
49	3.3533	0.2982	94.1310	28.0714	0.0106
50	3.4371	0.2909	97.4842	28.3623	0.0103

3%

PERIOD	TABLE 12-1 COMPOUND VALUE OF $1	TABLE 12-3 PRESENT VALUE OF $1	TABLE 13-1 AMOUNT OF ANNUITY OF $1	TABLE 13-2 PRESENT VALUE OF ANNUITY OF $1	TABLE 13-3 SINKING FUND VALUE OF $1
1	1.0300	0.9709	1.0000	0.9709	1.0000
2	1.0609	0.9426	2.0300	1.9135	0.4926
3	1.0927	0.9151	3.0909	2.8286	0.3235
4	1.1255	0.8885	4.1836	3.7171	0.2390
5	1.1593	0.8626	5.3091	4.5797	0.1884
6	1.1941	0.8375	6.4684	5.4172	0.1546
7	1.2299	0.8131	7.6625	6.2303	0.1305
8	1.2668	0.7894	8.8923	7.0197	0.1125
9	1.3048	0.7664	10.1591	7.7861	0.0984
10	1.3439	0.7441	11.4639	8.5302	0.0872
11	1.3842	0.7224	12.8078	9.2526	0.0781
12	1.4258	0.7014	14.1920	9.9540	0.0705
13	1.4685	0.6810	15.6178	10.6350	0.0640
14	1.5126	0.6611	17.0863	11.2961	0.0585
15	1.5580	0.6419	18.5989	11.9379	0.0538
16	1.6047	0.6232	20.1569	12.5611	0.0496
17	1.6528	0.6050	21.7616	13.1661	0.0460
18	1.7024	0.5874	23.4144	13.7535	0.0427
19	1.7535	0.5703	25.1169	14.3238	0.0398
20	1.8061	0.5537	26.8704	14.8775	0.0372
21	1.8603	0.5375	28.6765	15.4150	0.0349
22	1.9161	0.5219	30.5368	15.9369	0.0327
23	1.9736	0.5067	32.4529	16.4436	0.0308
24	2.0328	0.4919	34.4265	16.9355	0.0290
25	2.0938	0.4776	36.4593	17.4131	0.0274
26	2.1566	0.4637	38.5530	17.8768	0.0259
27	2.2213	0.4502	40.7096	18.3270	0.0246
28	2.2879	0.4371	42.9309	18.7641	0.0233
29	2.3566	0.4243	45.2188	19.1885	0.0221
30	2.4273	0.4120	47.5754	19.6004	0.0210
31	2.5001	0.4000	50.0027	20.0004	0.0200
32	2.5751	0.3883	52.5027	20.3888	0.0190
33	2.6523	0.3770	55.0778	20.7658	0.0182
34	2.7319	0.3660	57.7302	21.1318	0.0173
35	2.8139	0.3554	60.4621	21.4872	0.0165
36	2.8983	0.3450	63.2759	21.8323	0.0158
37	2.9852	0.3350	66.1742	22.1672	0.0151
38	3.0748	0.3252	69.1594	22.4925	0.0145
39	3.1670	0.3158	72.2342	22.8082	0.0138
40	3.2620	0.3066	75.4012	23.1148	0.0133
41	3.3599	0.2976	78.6633	23.4124	0.0127
42	3.4607	0.2890	82.0232	23.7014	0.0122
43	3.5645	0.2805	85.4839	23.9819	0.0117
44	3.6715	0.2724	89.0484	24.2543	0.0112
45	3.7816	0.2644	92.7198	24.5187	0.0108
46	3.8950	0.2567	96.5014	24.7754	0.0104
47	4.0119	0.2493	100.3965	25.0247	0.0100
48	4.1323	0.2420	104.4084	25.2667	0.0096
49	4.2562	0.2350	108.5406	25.5017	0.0092
50	4.3839	0.2281	112.7968	25.7298	0.0089

3½%

PERIOD	TABLE 12-1 COMPOUND VALUE OF $1	TABLE 12-3 PRESENT VALUE OF $1	TABLE 13-1 AMOUNT OF ANNUITY OF $1	TABLE 13-2 PRESENT VALUE OF ANNUITY OF $1	TABLE 13-3 SINKING FUND VALUE OF $1
1	1.0350	0.9662	1.0000	0.9662	1.0000
2	1.0712	0.9335	2.0350	1.8997	0.4914
3	1.1087	0.9019	3.1062	2.8016	0.3219
4	1.1475	0.8714	4.2149	3.6731	0.2373
5	1.1877	0.8420	5.3625	4.5150	0.1865
6	1.2293	0.8135	6.5501	5.3285	0.1527
7	1.2723	0.7860	7.7794	6.1145	0.1285
8	1.3168	0.7594	9.0517	6.8739	0.1105
9	1.3629	0.7337	10.3685	7.6077	0.0964
10	1.4106	0.7089	11.7314	8.3166	0.0852
11	1.4600	0.6849	13.1420	9.0015	0.0761
12	1.5111	0.6618	14.6019	9.6633	0.0685
13	1.5640	0.6394	16.1130	10.3027	0.0621
14	1.6187	0.6178	17.6770	10.9205	0.0566
15	1.6753	0.5969	19.2957	11.5174	0.0518
16	1.7340	0.5767	20.9710	12.0941	0.0477
17	1.7947	0.5572	22.7050	12.6513	0.0440
18	1.8575	0.5384	24.4997	13.1897	0.0408
19	1.9225	0.5202	26.3571	13.7098	0.0379
20	1.9898	0.5026	28.2796	14.2124	0.0354
21	2.0594	0.4856	30.2694	14.6980	0.0330
22	2.1315	0.4692	32.3288	15.1671	0.0309
23	2.2061	0.4533	34.4604	15.6204	0.0290
24	2.2833	0.4380	36.6665	16.0584	0.0273
25	2.3632	0.4231	38.9498	16.4815	0.0257
26	2.4460	0.4088	41.3130	16.8903	0.0242
27	2.5316	0.3950	43.7590	17.2854	0.0229
28	2.6202	0.3817	46.2905	17.6670	0.0216
29	2.7119	0.3687	48.9107	18.0358	0.0204
30	2.8068	0.3563	51.6226	18.3920	0.0194
31	2.9050	0.3442	54.4294	18.7363	0.0184
32	3.0067	0.3326	57.3344	19.0689	0.0174
33	3.1119	0.3213	60.3411	19.3902	0.0166
34	3.2209	0.3105	63.4530	19.7007	0.0158
35	3.3336	0.3000	66.6739	20.0007	0.0150
36	3.4503	0.2898	70.0075	20.2905	0.0143
37	3.5710	0.2800	73.4577	20.5705	0.0136
38	3.6960	0.2706	77.0287	20.8411	0.0130
39	3.8254	0.2614	80.7247	21.1025	0.0124
40	3.9593	0.2526	84.5501	21.3551	0.0118
41	4.0978	0.2440	88.5093	21.5991	0.0113
42	4.2413	0.2358	92.6072	21.8349	0.0108
43	4.3897	0.2278	96.8484	22.0627	0.0103
44	4.5433	0.2201	101.2381	22.2828	0.0099
45	4.7023	0.2127	105.7814	22.4954	0.0095
46	4.8669	0.2055	110.4838	22.7009	0.0091
47	5.0373	0.1985	115.3507	22.8994	0.0087
48	5.2136	0.1918	120.3880	23.0912	0.0083
49	5.3961	0.1853	125.6015	23.2766	0.0080
50	5.5849	0.1791	130.9976	23.4556	0.0076

7

4%

PERIOD	TABLE 12-1 COMPOUND VALUE OF $1	TABLE 12-3 PRESENT VALUE OF $1	TABLE 13-1 AMOUNT OF ANNUITY OF $1	TABLE 13-2 PRESENT VALUE OF ANNUITY OF $1	TABLE 13-3 SINKING FUND VALUE OF $1
1	1.0400	0.9615	1.0000	0.9615	1.0000
2	1.0816	0.9246	2.0400	1.8861	0.4902
3	1.1249	0.8890	3.1216	2.7751	0.3203
4	1.1699	0.8548	4.2465	3.6299	0.2355
5	1.2167	0.8219	5.4163	4.4518	0.1846
6	1.2653	0.7903	6.6330	5.2421	0.1508
7	1.3159	0.7599	7.8983	6.0021	0.1266
8	1.3686	0.7307	9.2142	6.7327	0.1085
9	1.4233	0.7026	10.5828	7.4353	0.0945
10	1.4802	0.6756	12.0061	8.1109	0.0833
11	1.5395	0.6496	13.4863	8.7605	0.0741
12	1.6010	0.6246	15.0258	9.3851	0.0666
13	1.6651	0.6006	16.6268	9.9856	0.0601
14	1.7317	0.5775	18.2919	10.5631	0.0547
15	1.8009	0.5553	20.0236	11.1184	0.0499
16	1.8730	0.5339	21.8245	11.6523	0.0458
17	1.9479	0.5134	23.6975	12.1657	0.0422
18	2.0258	0.4936	25.6454	12.6593	0.0390
19	2.1068	0.4746	27.6712	13.1339	0.0361
20	2.1911	0.4564	29.7781	13.5903	0.0336
21	2.2788	0.4388	31.9692	14.0292	0.0313
22	2.3699	0.4220	34.2479	14.4511	0.0292
23	2.4647	0.4057	36.6179	14.8568	0.0273
24	2.5633	0.3901	39.0826	15.2470	0.0256
25	2.6658	0.3751	41.6459	15.6221	0.0240
26	2.7725	0.3607	44.3117	15.9828	0.0226
27	2.8834	0.3468	47.0842	16.3296	0.0212
28	2.9987	0.3335	49.9675	16.6631	0.0200
29	3.1187	0.3207	52.9662	16.9837	0.0189
30	3.2434	0.3083	56.0849	17.2920	0.0178
31	3.3731	0.2965	59.3283	17.5885	0.0169
32	3.5081	0.2851	62.7014	17.8735	0.0159
33	3.6484	0.2741	66.2095	18.1476	0.0151
34	3.7943	0.2636	69.8578	18.4112	0.0143
35	3.9461	0.2534	73.6521	18.6646	0.0136
36	4.1039	0.2437	77.5982	18.9083	0.0129
37	4.2681	0.2343	81.7022	19.1426	0.0122
38	4.4388	0.2253	85.9702	19.3679	0.0116
39	4.6164	0.2166	90.4091	19.5845	0.0111
40	4.8010	0.2083	95.0254	19.7928	0.0105
41	4.9931	0.2003	99.8264	19.9930	0.0100
42	5.1928	0.1926	104.8195	20.1856	0.0095
43	5.4005	0.1852	110.0122	20.3708	0.0091
44	5.6165	0.1780	115.4127	20.5488	0.0087
45	5.8412	0.1712	121.0292	20.7200	0.0083
46	6.0748	0.1646	126.8704	20.8847	0.0079
47	6.3178	0.1583	132.9452	21.0429	0.0075
48	6.5705	0.1522	139.2630	21.1951	0.0072
49	6.8333	0.1463	145.8335	21.3415	0.0069
50	7.1067	0.1407	152.6669	21.4822	0.0066

PERIOD	TABLE 12-1 COMPOUND VALUE OF $1	TABLE 12-3 PRESENT VALUE OF $1	TABLE 13-1 AMOUNT OF ANNUITY OF $1	TABLE 13-2 PRESENT VALUE OF ANNUITY OF $1	TABLE 13-3 SINKING FUND VALUE OF $1
1	1.0450	0.9569	1.0000	0.9569	1.0000
2	1.0920	0.9157	2.0450	1.8727	0.4890
3	1.1412	0.8763	3.1370	2.7490	0.3188
4	1.1925	0.8386	4.2782	3.5875	0.2337
5	1.2462	0.8025	5.4707	4.3900	0.1828
6	1.3023	0.7679	6.7169	5.1579	0.1489
7	1.3609	0.7348	8.0191	5.8927	0.1247
8	1.4221	0.7032	9.3800	6.5959	0.1066
9	1.4861	0.6729	10.8021	7.2688	0.0926
10	1.5530	0.6439	12.2882	7.9127	0.0814
11	1.6229	0.6162	13.8412	8.5289	0.0722
12	1.6959	0.5897	15.4640	9.1186	0.0647
13	1.7722	0.5643	17.1599	9.6828	0.0583
14	1.8519	0.5400	18.9321	10.2228	0.0528
15	1.9353	0.5167	20.7840	10.7395	0.0481
16	2.0224	0.4945	22.7193	11.2340	0.0440
17	2.1134	0.4732	24.7417	11.7072	0.0404
18	2.2085	0.4528	26.8551	12.1600	0.0372
19	2.3079	0.4333	29.0635	12.5933	0.0344
20	2.4117	0.4146	31.3714	13.0079	0.0319
21	2.5202	0.3968	33.7831	13.4047	0.0296
22	2.6337	0.3797	36.3033	13.7844	0.0275
23	2.7522	0.3634	38.9370	14.1478	0.0257
24	2.8760	0.3477	41.6892	14.4955	0.0240
25	3.0054	0.3327	44.5652	14.8282	0.0224
26	3.1407	0.3184	47.5706	15.1466	0.0210
27	3.2820	0.3047	50.7113	15.4513	0.0197
28	3.4297	0.2916	53.9933	15.7429	0.0185
29	3.5840	0.2790	57.4230	16.0219	0.0174
30	3.7453	0.2670	61.0070	16.2889	0.0164
31	3.9139	0.2555	64.7523	16.5444	0.0154
32	4.0900	0.2445	68.6662	16.7889	0.0146
33	4.2740	0.2340	72.7562	17.0229	0.0137
34	4.4664	0.2239	77.0302	17.2468	0.0130
35	4.6673	0.2143	81.4965	17.4610	0.0123
36	4.8774	0.2050	86.1639	17.6660	0.0116
37	5.0969	0.1962	91.0412	17.8622	0.0110
38	5.3262	0.1878	96.1381	18.0500	0.0104
39	5.5659	0.1797	101.4643	18.2297	0.0099
40	5.8164	0.1719	107.0302	18.4016	0.0093
41	6.0781	0.1645	112.8466	18.5661	0.0089
42	6.3516	0.1574	118.9247	18.7235	0.0084
43	6.6374	0.1507	125.2763	18.8742	0.0080
44	6.9361	0.1442	131.9137	19.0184	0.0076
45	7.2482	0.1380	138.8498	19.1563	0.0072
46	7.5744	0.1320	146.0980	19.2884	0.0068
47	7.9153	0.1263	153.6724	19.4147	0.0065
48	8.2714	0.1209	161.5877	19.5356	0.0062
49	8.6437	0.1157	169.8592	19.6513	0.0059
50	9.0326	0.1107	178.5028	19.7620	0.0056

5%

PERIOD	TABLE 12-1 COMPOUND VALUE OF $1	TABLE 12-3 PRESENT VALUE OF $1	TABLE 13-1 AMOUNT OF ANNUITY OF $1	TABLE 13-2 PRESENT VALUE OF ANNUITY OF $1	TABLE 13-3 SINKING FUND VALUE OF $1
1	1.0500	0.9524	1.0000	0.9524	1.0000
2	1.1025	0.9070	2.0500	1.8594	0.4878
3	1.1576	0.8638	3.1525	2.7232	0.3172
4	1.2155	0.8227	4.3101	3.5459	0.2320
5	1.2763	0.7835	5.5256	4.3295	0.1810
6	1.3401	0.7462	6.8019	5.0757	0.1470
7	1.4071	0.7107	8.1420	5.7864	0.1228
8	1.4775	0.6768	9.5491	6.4632	0.1047
9	1.5513	0.6446	11.0265	7.1078	0.0907
10	1.6289	0.6139	12.5779	7.7217	0.0795
11	1.7103	0.5847	14.2068	8.3064	0.0704
12	1.7959	0.5568	15.9171	8.8632	0.0628
13	1.8856	0.5303	17.7129	9.3936	0.0565
14	1.9799	0.5051	19.5986	9.8986	0.0510
15	2.0789	0.4810	21.5785	10.3796	0.0463
16	2.1829	0.4581	23.6574	10.8378	0.0423
17	2.2920	0.4363	25.8403	11.2741	0.0387
18	2.4066	0.4155	28.1323	11.6896	0.0355
19	2.5270	0.3957	30.5389	12.0853	0.0327
20	2.6533	0.3769	33.0659	12.4622	0.0302
21	2.7860	0.3589	35.7192	12.8211	0.0280
22	2.9253	0.3418	38.5051	13.1630	0.0260
23	3.0715	0.3256	41.4304	13.4886	0.0241
24	3.2251	0.3101	44.5019	13.7986	0.0225
25	3.3864	0.2953	47.7270	14.0939	0.0210
26	3.5557	0.2812	51.1133	14.3752	0.0196
27	3.7335	0.2678	54.6690	14.6430	0.0183
28	3.9201	0.2551	58.4024	14.8981	0.0171
29	4.1161	0.2429	62.3225	15.1411	0.0160
30	4.3219	0.2314	66.4386	15.3724	0.0151
31	4.5380	0.2204	70.7606	15.5928	0.0141
32	4.7649	0.2099	75.2986	15.8027	0.0133
33	5.0032	0.1999	80.0635	16.0025	0.0125
34	5.2533	0.1904	85.0667	16.1929	0.0118
35	5.5160	0.1813	90.3200	16.3742	0.0111
36	5.7918	0.1727	95.8360	16.5468	0.0104
37	6.0814	0.1644	101.6278	16.7113	0.0098
38	6.3855	0.1566	107.7092	16.8679	0.0093
39	6.7047	0.1491	114.0946	17.0170	0.0088
40	7.0400	0.1420	120.7993	17.1591	0.0083
41	7.3920	0.1353	127.8393	17.2944	0.0078
42	7.7616	0.1288	135.2312	17.4232	0.0074
43	8.1496	0.1227	142.9928	17.5459	0.0070
44	8.5571	0.1169	151.1424	17.6628	0.0066
45	8.9850	0.1113	159.6995	17.7741	0.0063
46	9.4342	0.1060	168.6845	17.8801	0.0059
47	9.9059	0.1009	178.1187	17.9810	0.0056
48	10.4012	0.0961	188.0246	18.0772	0.0053
49	10.9213	0.0916	198.4258	18.1687	0.0050
50	11.4674	0.0872	209.3470	18.2559	0.0048

$5\frac{1}{2}\%$

PERIOD	TABLE 12-1 COMPOUND VALUE OF $1	TABLE 12-3 PRESENT VALUE OF $1	TABLE 13-1 AMOUNT OF ANNUITY OF $1	TABLE 13-2 PRESENT VALUE OF ANNUITY OF $1	TABLE 13-3 SINKING FUND VALUE OF $1
1	1.0550	0.9479	1.0000	0.9479	1.0000
2	1.1130	0.8985	2.0550	1.8463	0.4866
3	1.1742	0.8516	3.1680	2.6979	0.3157
4	1.2388	0.8072	4.3423	3.5051	0.2303
5	1.3070	0.7651	5.5811	4.2703	0.1792
6	1.3788	0.7252	6.8880	4.9955	0.1452
7	1.4547	0.6874	8.2669	5.6830	0.1210
8	1.5347	0.6516	9.7216	6.3346	0.1029
9	1.6191	0.6176	11.2562	6.9522	0.0888
10	1.7081	0.5854	12.8753	7.5376	0.0777
11	1.8021	0.5549	14.5835	8.0925	0.0686
12	1.9012	0.5260	16.3856	8.6185	0.0610
13	2.0058	0.4986	18.2868	9.1171	0.0547
14	2.1161	0.4726	20.2925	9.5896	0.0493
15	2.2325	0.4479	22.4086	10.0376	0.0446
16	2.3553	0.4246	24.6411	10.4622	0.0406
17	2.4848	0.4024	26.9963	10.8646	0.0370
18	2.6215	0.3815	29.4811	11.2461	0.0339
19	2.7656	0.3616	32.1026	11.6076	0.0312
20	2.9178	0.3427	34.8682	11.9504	0.0287
21	3.0782	0.3249	37.7860	12.2752	0.0265
22	3.2475	0.3079	40.8642	12.5832	0.0245
23	3.4261	0.2919	44.1117	12.8750	0.0227
24	3.6146	0.2767	47.5379	13.1517	0.0210
25	3.8134	0.2622	51.1524	13.4139	0.0195
26	4.0231	0.2486	54.9658	13.6625	0.0182
27	4.2444	0.2356	58.9889	13.8981	0.0170
28	4.4778	0.2233	63.2333	14.1214	0.0158
29	4.7241	0.2117	67.7112	14.3331	0.0148
30	4.9839	0.2006	72.4353	14.5337	0.0138
31	5.2581	0.1902	77.4192	14.7239	0.0129
32	5.5472	0.1803	82.6772	14.9042	0.0121
33	5.8523	0.1709	88.2245	15.0751	0.0113
34	6.1742	0.1620	94.0768	15.2370	0.0106
35	6.5138	0.1535	100.2510	15.3905	0.0100
36	6.8721	0.1455	106.7648	15.5361	0.0094
37	7.2500	0.1379	113.6369	15.6740	0.0088
38	7.6488	0.1307	120.8869	15.8047	0.0083
39	8.0695	0.1239	128.5357	15.9287	0.0078
40	8.5133	0.1175	136.6051	16.0461	0.0073
41	8.9815	0.1113	145.1184	16.1575	0.0069
42	9.4755	0.1055	154.0999	16.2630	0.0065
43	9.9966	0.1000	163.5753	16.3630	0.0061
44	10.5465	0.0948	173.5720	16.4578	0.0058
45	11.1265	0.0899	184.1184	16.5477	0.0054
46	11.7385	0.0852	195.2449	16.6329	0.0051
47	12.3841	0.0807	206.9834	16.7137	0.0048
48	13.0652	0.0765	219.3674	16.7902	0.0046
49	13.7838	0.0725	232.4326	16.8627	0.0043
50	14.5419	0.0688	246.2164	16.9315	0.0041

11

6%

PERIOD	TABLE 12-1 COMPOUND VALUE OF $1	TABLE 12-3 PRESENT VALUE OF $1	TABLE 13-1 AMOUNT OF ANNUITY OF $1	TABLE 13-2 PRESENT VALUE OF ANNUITY OF $1	TABLE 13-3 SINKING FUND VALUE OF $1
1	1.0600	0.9434	1.0000	0.9434	1.0000
2	1.1236	0.8900	2.0600	1.8334	0.4854
3	1.1910	0.8396	3.1836	2.6730	0.3141
4	1.2625	0.7921	4.3746	3.4651	0.2286
5	1.3382	0.7473	5.6371	4.2124	0.1774
6	1.4185	0.7050	6.9753	4.9173	0.1434
7	1.5036	0.6651	8.3938	5.5824	0.1191
8	1.5938	0.6274	9.8975	6.2098	0.1010
9	1.6895	0.5919	11.4913	6.8017	0.0870
10	1.7908	0.5584	13.1808	7.3601	0.0759
11	1.8983	0.5268	14.9716	7.8869	0.0668
12	2.0122	0.4970	16.8699	8.3838	0.0593
13	2.1329	0.4688	18.8821	8.8527	0.0530
14	2.2609	0.4423	21.0150	9.2950	0.0476
15	2.3966	0.4173	23.2759	9.7122	0.0430
16	2.5404	0.3936	25.6725	10.1059	0.0390
17	2.6928	0.3714	28.2128	10.4773	0.0354
18	2.8543	0.3503	30.9056	10.8276	0.0324
19	3.0256	0.3305	33.7599	11.1581	0.0296
20	3.2071	0.3118	36.7855	11.4699	0.0272
21	3.3996	0.2942	39.9927	11.7641	0.0250
22	3.6035	0.2775	43.3922	12.0416	0.0230
23	3.8197	0.2618	46.9958	12.3034	0.0213
24	4.0489	0.2470	50.8155	12.5504	0.0197
25	4.2919	0.2330	54.8644	12.7834	0.0182
26	4.5494	0.2198	59.1563	13.0032	0.0169
27	4.8223	0.2074	63.7057	13.2105	0.0157
28	5.1117	0.1956	68.5280	13.4062	0.0146
29	5.4184	0.1846	73.6397	13.5907	0.0136
30	5.7435	0.1741	79.0580	13.7648	0.0126
31	6.0881	0.1643	84.8015	13.9291	0.0118
32	6.4534	0.1550	90.8896	14.0840	0.0110
33	6.8406	0.1462	97.3430	14.2302	0.0103
34	7.2510	0.1379	104.1836	14.3681	0.0096
35	7.6861	0.1301	111.4346	14.4982	0.0090
36	8.1472	0.1227	119.1206	14.6210	0.0084
37	8.6361	0.1158	127.2679	14.7368	0.0079
38	9.1542	0.1092	135.9039	14.8460	0.0074
39	9.7035	0.1031	145.0581	14.9491	0.0069
40	10.2857	0.0972	154.7616	15.0463	0.0065
41	10.9028	0.0917	165.0473	15.1380	0.0061
42	11.5570	0.0865	175.9501	15.2245	0.0057
43	12.2504	0.0816	187.5071	15.3062	0.0053
44	12.9855	0.0770	199.7575	15.3832	0.0050
45	13.7646	0.0727	212.7430	15.4558	0.0047
46	14.5905	0.0685	226.5076	15.5244	0.0044
47	15.4659	0.0647	241.0980	15.5890	0.0041
48	16.3938	0.0610	256.5639	15.6500	0.0039
49	17.3775	0.0575	272.9577	15.7076	0.0037
50	18.4201	0.0543	290.3351	15.7619	0.0034

PERIOD	TABLE 12-1 COMPOUND VALUE OF $1	TABLE 12-3 PRESENT VALUE OF $1	TABLE 13-1 AMOUNT OF ANNUITY OF $1	TABLE 13-2 PRESENT VALUE OF ANNUITY OF $1	TABLE 13-3 SINKING FUND VALUE OF $1
1	1.0650	0.9390	1.0000	0.9390	1.0000
2	1.1342	0.8817	2.0650	1.8206	0.4843
3	1.2079	0.8278	3.1992	2.6485	0.3126
4	1.2865	0.7773	4.4072	3.4258	0.2269
5	1.3701	0.7299	5.6936	4.1557	0.1756
6	1.4591	0.6853	7.0637	4.8410	0.1416
7	1.5540	0.6435	8.5229	5.4845	0.1173
8	1.6550	0.6042	10.0768	6.0887	0.0992
9	1.7626	0.5674	11.7318	6.6561	0.0852
10	1.8771	0.5327	13.4944	7.1888	0.0741
11	1.9992	0.5002	15.3715	7.6890	0.0651
12	2.1291	0.4697	17.3707	8.1587	0.0576
13	2.2675	0.4410	19.4998	8.5997	0.0513
14	2.4149	0.4141	21.7673	9.0138	0.0459
15	2.5718	0.3888	24.1821	9.4027	0.0414
16	2.7390	0.3651	26.7540	9.7678	0.0374
17	2.9170	0.3428	29.4930	10.1106	0.0339
18	3.1067	0.3219	32.4100	10.4325	0.0309
19	3.3086	0.3022	35.5167	10.7347	0.0282
20	3.5236	0.2838	38.8253	11.0185	0.0258
21	3.7527	0.2665	42.3489	11.2850	0.0236
22	3.9966	0.2502	46.1016	11.5352	0.0217
23	4.2564	0.2349	50.0982	11.7701	0.0200
24	4.5330	0.2206	54.3546	11.9907	0.0184
25	4.8277	0.2071	58.8876	12.1979	0.0170
26	5.1415	0.1945	63.7153	12.3924	0.0157
27	5.4757	0.1826	68.8568	12.5750	0.0145
28	5.8316	0.1715	74.3325	12.7465	0.0135
29	6.2107	0.1610	80.1641	12.9075	0.0125
30	6.6144	0.1512	86.3747	13.0587	0.0116
31	7.0443	0.1420	92.9891	13.2006	0.0108
32	7.5022	0.1333	100.0334	13.3339	0.0100
33	7.9898	0.1252	107.5355	13.4591	0.0093
34	8.5091	0.1175	115.5254	13.5766	0.0087
35	9.0622	0.1103	124.0345	13.6870	0.0081
36	9.6513	0.1036	133.0967	13.7906	0.0075
37	10.2786	0.0973	142.7480	13.8879	0.0070
38	10.9467	0.0914	153.0266	13.9792	0.0065
39	11.6583	0.0858	163.9733	14.0650	0.0061
40	12.4161	0.0805	175.6316	14.1455	0.0057
41	13.2231	0.0756	188.0476	14.2212	0.0053
42	14.0826	0.0710	201.2707	14.2922	0.0050
43	14.9980	0.0667	215.3533	14.3588	0.0046
44	15.9728	0.0626	230.3513	14.4214	0.0043
45	17.0111	0.0588	246.3241	14.4802	0.0041
46	18.1168	0.0552	263.3352	14.5354	0.0038
47	19.2944	0.0518	281.4519	14.5873	0.0036
48	20.5485	0.0487	300.7463	14.6359	0.0033
49	21.8842	0.0457	321.2948	14.6816	0.0031
50	23.3066	0.0429	343.1789	14.7245	0.0029

7%

PERIOD	TABLE 12-1 COMPOUND VALUE OF $1	TABLE 12-3 PRESENT VALUE OF $1	TABLE 13-1 AMOUNT OF ANNUITY OF $1	TABLE 13-2 PRESENT VALUE OF ANNUITY OF $1	TABLE 13-3 SINKING FUND VALUE OF $1
1	1.0700	0.9346	1.0000	0.9346	1.0000
2	1.1449	0.8734	2.0700	1.8080	0.4831
3	1.2250	0.8163	3.2149	2.6243	0.3111
4	1.3108	0.7629	4.4399	3.3872	0.2252
5	1.4026	0.7130	5.7507	4.1002	0.1739
6	1.5007	0.6663	7.1533	4.7665	0.1398
7	1.6058	0.6227	8.6540	5.3893	0.1156
8	1.7182	0.5820	10.2598	5.9713	0.0975
9	1.8385	0.5439	11.9780	6.5152	0.0835
10	1.9672	0.5083	13.8164	7.0236	0.0724
11	2.1049	0.4751	15.7836	7.4987	0.0634
12	2.2522	0.4440	17.8884	7.9427	0.0559
13	2.4098	0.4150	20.1406	8.3576	0.0497
14	2.5785	0.3878	22.5505	8.7455	0.0443
15	2.7590	0.3624	25.1290	9.1079	0.0398
16	2.9522	0.3387	27.8880	9.4466	0.0359
17	3.1588	0.3166	30.8402	9.7632	0.0324
18	3.3799	0.2959	33.9990	10.0591	0.0294
19	3.6165	0.2765	37.3789	10.3356	0.0268
20	3.8697	0.2584	40.9954	10.5940	0.0244
21	4.1406	0.2415	44.8651	10.8355	0.0223
22	4.4304	0.2257	49.0057	11.0612	0.0204
23	4.7405	0.2109	53.4360	11.2722	0.0187
24	5.0724	0.1971	58.1766	11.4693	0.0172
25	5.4274	0.1842	63.2489	11.6536	0.0158
26	5.8074	0.1722	68.6763	11.8258	0.0146
27	6.2139	0.1609	74.4837	11.9867	0.0134
28	6.6488	0.1504	80.6975	12.1371	0.0124
29	7.1143	0.1406	87.3464	12.2777	0.0114
30	7.6123	0.1314	94.4606	12.4090	0.0106
31	8.1451	0.1228	102.0728	12.5318	0.0098
32	8.7153	0.1147	110.2179	12.6466	0.0091
33	9.3253	0.1072	118.9332	12.7538	0.0084
34	9.9781	0.1002	128.2585	12.8540	0.0078
35	10.6766	0.0937	138.2366	12.9477	0.0072
36	11.4239	0.0875	148.9131	13.0352	0.0067
37	12.2236	0.0818	160.3370	13.1170	0.0062
38	13.0792	0.0765	172.5606	13.1935	0.0058
39	13.9948	0.0715	185.6398	13.2649	0.0054
40	14.9744	0.0668	199.6346	13.3317	0.0050
41	16.0226	0.0624	214.6090	13.3941	0.0047
42	17.1442	0.0583	230.6317	13.4524	0.0043
43	18.3443	0.0545	247.7758	13.5070	0.0040
44	19.6284	0.0509	266.1201	13.5579	0.0038
45	21.0024	0.0476	285.7485	13.6055	0.0035
46	22.4726	0.0445	306.7509	13.6500	0.0033
47	24.0456	0.0416	329.2234	13.6916	0.0030
48	25.7288	0.0389	353.2691	13.7305	0.0028
49	27.5298	0.0363	378.9978	13.7668	0.0026
50	29.4569	0.0339	406.5277	13.8007	0.0025

$7\tfrac{1}{2}\%$

PERIOD	TABLE 12-1 COMPOUND VALUE OF $1	TABLE 12-3 PRESENT VALUE OF $1	TABLE 13-1 AMOUNT OF ANNUITY OF $1	TABLE 13-2 PRESENT VALUE OF ANNUITY OF $1	TABLE 13-3 SINKING FUND VALUE OF $1
1	1.0750	0.9302	1.0000	0.9302	1.0000
2	1.1556	0.8653	2.0750	1.7956	0.4819
3	1.2423	0.8050	3.2306	2.6005	0.3095
4	1.3355	0.7488	4.4729	3.3493	0.2236
5	1.4356	0.6966	5.8084	4.0459	0.1722
6	1.5433	0.6480	7.2440	4.6938	0.1380
7	1.6590	0.6028	8.7873	5.2966	0.1138
8	1.7835	0.5607	10.4464	5.8573	0.0957
9	1.9172	0.5216	12.2299	6.3789	0.0818
10	2.0610	0.4852	14.1471	6.8641	0.0707
11	2.2156	0.4513	16.2081	7.3154	0.0617
12	2.3818	0.4199	18.4237	7.7353	0.0543
13	2.5604	0.3906	20.8055	8.1258	0.0481
14	2.7524	0.3633	23.3659	8.4892	0.0428
15	2.9589	0.3380	26.1184	8.8271	0.0383
16	3.1808	0.3144	29.0773	9.1415	0.0344
17	3.4194	0.2925	32.2581	9.4340	0.0310
18	3.6758	0.2720	35.6774	9.7060	0.0280
19	3.9515	0.2531	39.3532	9.9591	0.0254
20	4.2479	0.2354	43.3047	10.1945	0.0231
21	4.5664	0.2190	47.5526	10.4135	0.0210
22	4.9089	0.2037	52.1190	10.6172	0.0192
23	5.2771	0.1895	57.0280	10.8067	0.0175
24	5.6729	0.1763	62.3051	10.9830	0.0161
25	6.0983	0.1640	67.9780	11.1469	0.0147
26	6.5557	0.1525	74.0763	11.2995	0.0135
27	7.0474	0.1419	80.6320	11.4414	0.0124
28	7.5760	0.1320	87.6794	11.5734	0.0114
29	8.1442	0.1228	95.2554	11.6962	0.0105
30	8.7550	0.1142	103.3996	11.8104	0.0097
31	9.4116	0.1063	112.1545	11.9166	0.0089
32	10.1175	0.0988	121.5661	12.0155	0.0082
33	10.8763	0.0919	131.6836	12.1074	0.0076
34	11.6920	0.0855	142.5599	12.1930	0.0070
35	12.5689	0.0796	154.2519	12.2725	0.0065
36	13.5116	0.0740	166.8208	12.3465	0.0060
37	14.5249	0.0688	180.3323	12.4154	0.0055
38	15.6143	0.0640	194.8573	12.4794	0.0051
39	16.7854	0.0596	210.4716	12.5390	0.0048
40	18.0443	0.0554	227.2569	12.5944	0.0044
41	19.3976	0.0516	245.3012	12.6460	0.0041
42	20.8524	0.0480	264.6988	12.6939	0.0038
43	22.4163	0.0446	285.5513	12.7385	0.0035
44	24.0976	0.0415	307.9676	12.7800	0.0032
45	25.9049	0.0386	332.0652	12.8186	0.0030
46	27.8478	0.0359	357.9701	12.8545	0.0028
47	29.9363	0.0334	385.8179	12.8879	0.0026
48	32.1816	0.0311	415.7542	12.9190	0.0024
49	34.5952	0.0289	447.9358	12.9479	0.0022
50	37.1898	0.0269	482.5310	12.9748	0.0021

8%

PERIOD	TABLE 12-1 COMPOUND VALUE OF $1	TABLE 12-3 PRESENT VALUE OF $1	TABLE 13-1 AMOUNT OF ANNUITY OF $1	TABLE 13-2 PRESENT VALUE OF ANNUITY OF $1	TABLE 13-3 SINKING FUND VALUE OF $1
1	1.0800	0.9259	1.0000	0.9259	1.0000
2	1.1664	0.8573	2.0800	1.7833	0.4808
3	1.2597	0.7938	3.2464	2.5771	0.3080
4	1.3605	0.7350	4.5061	3.3121	0.2219
5	1.4693	0.6806	5.8666	3.9927	0.1705
6	1.5869	0.6302	7.3359	4.6229	0.1363
7	1.7138	0.5835	8.9228	5.2064	0.1121
8	1.8509	0.5403	10.6366	5.7466	0.0940
9	1.9990	0.5002	12.4876	6.2469	0.0801
10	2.1589	0.4632	14.4866	6.7101	0.0690
11	2.3316	0.4289	16.6455	7.1390	0.0601
12	2.5182	0.3971	18.9771	7.5361	0.0527
13	2.7196	0.3677	21.4953	7.9038	0.0465
14	2.9372	0.3405	24.2149	8.2442	0.0413
15	3.1722	0.3152	27.1521	8.5595	0.0368
16	3.4259	0.2919	30.3243	8.8514	0.0330
17	3.7000	0.2703	33.7503	9.1216	0.0296
18	3.9960	0.2502	37.4503	9.3719	0.0267
19	4.3157	0.2317	41.4463	9.6036	0.0241
20	4.6610	0.2145	45.7620	9.8181	0.0219
21	5.0338	0.1987	50.4230	10.0168	0.0198
22	5.4365	0.1839	55.4568	10.2007	0.0180
23	5.8715	0.1703	60.8933	10.3711	0.0164
24	6.3412	0.1577	66.7648	10.5288	0.0150
25	6.8485	0.1460	73.1060	10.6748	0.0137
26	7.3964	0.1352	79.9545	10.8100	0.0125
27	7.9881	0.1252	87.3509	10.9352	0.0114
28	8.6271	0.1159	95.3389	11.0511	0.0105
29	9.3173	0.1073	103.9660	11.1584	0.0096
30	10.0627	0.0994	113.2833	11.2578	0.0088
31	10.8677	0.0920	123.3460	11.3498	0.0081
32	11.7371	0.0852	134.2137	11.4350	0.0075
33	12.6761	0.0789	145.9508	11.5139	0.0069
34	13.6901	0.0730	158.6269	11.5869	0.0063
35	14.7854	0.0676	172.3170	11.6546	0.0058
36	15.9682	0.0626	187.1024	11.7172	0.0053
37	17.2456	0.0580	203.0706	11.7752	0.0049
38	18.6253	0.0537	220.3162	11.8289	0.0045
39	20.1153	0.0497	238.9415	11.8786	0.0042
40	21.7245	0.0460	259.0569	11.9246	0.0039
41	23.4625	0.0426	280.7814	11.9672	0.0036
42	25.3395	0.0395	304.2440	12.0067	0.0033
43	27.3667	0.0365	329.5835	12.0432	0.0030
44	29.5560	0.0338	356.9502	12.0771	0.0028
45	31.9205	0.0313	386.5062	12.1084	0.0026
46	34.4741	0.0290	418.4267	12.1374	0.0024
47	37.2321	0.0269	452.9009	12.1643	0.0022
48	40.2106	0.0249	490.1329	12.1891	0.0020
49	43.4275	0.0230	530.3436	12.2122	0.0019
50	46.9017	0.0213	573.7711	12.2335	0.0017

8½%

PERIOD	TABLE 12-1 COMPOUND VALUE OF $1	TABLE 12-3 PRESENT VALUE OF $1	TABLE 13-1 AMOUNT OF ANNUITY OF $1	TABLE 13-2 PRESENT VALUE OF ANNUITY OF $1	TABLE 13-3 SINKING FUND VALUE OF $1
1	1.0850	0.9217	1.0000	0.9217	1.0000
2	1.1772	0.8495	2.0850	1.7711	0.4796
3	1.2773	0.7829	3.2622	2.5540	0.3065
4	1.3859	0.7216	4.5395	3.2756	0.2203
5	1.5037	0.6650	5.9254	3.9406	0.1688
6	1.6315	0.6129	7.4290	4.5536	0.1346
7	1.7701	0.5649	9.0605	5.1185	0.1104
8	1.9206	0.5207	10.8307	5.6392	0.0923
9	2.0839	0.4799	12.7513	6.1191	0.0784
10	2.2610	0.4423	14.8351	6.5614	0.0674
11	2.4532	0.4076	17.0961	6.9690	0.0585
12	2.6617	0.3757	19.5493	7.3447	0.0512
13	2.8879	0.3463	22.2110	7.6910	0.0450
14	3.1334	0.3191	25.0989	8.0101	0.0398
15	3.3997	0.2941	28.2323	8.3042	0.0354
16	3.6887	0.2711	31.6321	8.5753	0.0316
17	4.0023	0.2499	35.3208	8.8252	0.0283
18	4.3425	0.2303	39.3230	9.0555	0.0254
19	4.7116	0.2122	43.6655	9.2677	0.0229
20	5.1121	0.1956	48.3771	9.4633	0.0207
21	5.5466	0.1803	53.4891	9.6436	0.0187
22	6.0180	0.1662	59.0357	9.8098	0.0169
23	6.5296	0.1531	65.0538	9.9629	0.0154
24	7.0846	0.1412	71.5833	10.1041	0.0140
25	7.6868	0.1301	78.6679	10.2342	0.0127
26	8.3401	0.1199	86.3547	10.3541	0.0116
27	9.0491	0.1105	94.6949	10.4646	0.0106
28	9.8182	0.1019	103.7439	10.5665	0.0096
29	10.6528	0.0939	113.5622	10.6603	0.0088
30	11.5583	0.0865	124.2149	10.7468	0.0081
31	12.5407	0.0797	135.7732	10.8266	0.0074
32	13.6067	0.0735	148.3140	10.9001	0.0067
33	14.7633	0.0677	161.9207	10.9678	0.0062
34	16.0181	0.0624	176.6839	11.0302	0.0057
35	17.3797	0.0575	192.7021	11.0878	0.0052
36	18.8569	0.0530	210.0818	11.1408	0.0048
37	20.4598	0.0489	228.9387	11.1897	0.0044
38	22.1989	0.0450	249.3985	11.2347	0.0040
39	24.0858	0.0415	271.5974	11.2763	0.0037
40	26.1331	0.0383	295.6832	11.3145	0.0034
41	28.3544	0.0353	321.8163	11.3498	0.0031
42	30.7645	0.0325	350.1707	11.3823	0.0029
43	33.3795	0.0300	380.9352	11.4123	0.0026
44	36.2168	0.0276	414.3148	11.4399	0.0024
45	39.2952	0.0254	450.5315	11.4653	0.0022
46	42.6353	0.0235	489.8267	11.4888	0.0020
47	46.2593	0.0216	532.4620	11.5104	0.0019
48	50.1913	0.0199	578.7213	11.5303	0.0017
49	54.4576	0.0184	628.9127	11.5487	0.0016
50	59.0865	0.0169	683.3703	11.5656	0.0015

9%

PERIOD	TABLE 12-1 COMPOUND VALUE OF $1	TABLE 12-3 PRESENT VALUE OF $1	TABLE 13-1 AMOUNT OF ANNUITY OF $1	TABLE 13-2 PRESENT VALUE OF ANNUITY OF $1	TABLE 13-3 SINKING FUND VALUE OF $1
1	1.0900	0.9174	1.0000	0.9174	1.0000
2	1.1881	0.8417	2.0900	1.7591	0.4785
3	1.2950	0.7722	3.2781	2.5313	0.3051
4	1.4116	0.7084	4.5731	3.2397	0.2187
5	1.5386	0.6499	5.9847	3.8897	0.1671
6	1.6771	0.5963	7.5233	4.4859	0.1329
7	1.8280	0.5470	9.2004	5.0330	0.1087
8	1.9926	0.5019	11.0285	5.5348	0.0907
9	2.1719	0.4604	13.0210	5.9952	0.0768
10	2.3674	0.4224	15.1929	6.4177	0.0658
11	2.5804	0.3875	17.5603	6.8052	0.0569
12	2.8127	0.3555	20.1407	7.1607	0.0497
13	3.0658	0.3262	22.9534	7.4869	0.0436
14	3.3417	0.2992	26.0192	7.7862	0.0384
15	3.6425	0.2745	29.3609	8.0607	0.0341
16	3.9703	0.2519	33.0034	8.3126	0.0303
17	4.3276	0.2311	36.9737	8.5436	0.0270
18	4.7171	0.2120	41.3014	8.7556	0.0242
19	5.1417	0.1945	46.0185	8.9501	0.0217
20	5.6044	0.1784	51.1602	9.1285	0.0195
21	6.1088	0.1637	56.7646	9.2922	0.0176
22	6.6586	0.1502	62.8734	9.4424	0.0159
23	7.2579	0.1378	69.5320	9.5802	0.0144
24	7.9111	0.1264	76.7899	9.7066	0.0130
25	8.6231	0.1160	84.7010	9.8226	0.0118
26	9.3992	0.1064	93.3241	9.9290	0.0107
27	10.2451	0.0976	102.7233	10.0266	0.0097
28	11.1672	0.0895	112.9684	10.1161	0.0089
29	12.1722	0.0822	124.1355	10.1983	0.0081
30	13.2677	0.0754	136.3077	10.2737	0.0073
31	14.4618	0.0691	149.5754	10.3428	0.0067
32	15.7634	0.0634	164.0372	10.4062	0.0061
33	17.1821	0.0582	179.8006	10.4644	0.0056
34	18.7284	0.0534	196.9827	10.5178	0.0051
35	20.4140	0.0490	215.7111	10.5668	0.0046
36	22.2513	0.0449	236.1251	10.6118	0.0042
37	24.2539	0.0412	258.3764	10.6530	0.0039
38	26.4367	0.0378	282.6303	10.6908	0.0035
39	28.8160	0.0347	309.0670	10.7255	0.0032
40	31.4095	0.0318	337.8831	10.7574	0.0030
41	34.2363	0.0292	369.2925	10.7866	0.0027
42	37.3176	0.0268	403.5289	10.8134	0.0025
43	40.6762	0.0246	440.8465	10.8380	0.0023
44	44.3371	0.0226	481.5228	10.8605	0.0021
45	48.3274	0.0207	525.8598	10.8812	0.0019
46	52.6769	0.0190	574.1872	10.9002	0.0017
47	57.4178	0.0174	626.8641	10.9176	0.0016
48	62.5854	0.0160	684.2819	10.9336	0.0015
49	68.2181	0.0147	746.8673	10.9482	0.0013
50	74.3577	0.0134	815.0853	10.9617	0.0012

PERIOD	TABLE 12-1 COMPOUND VALUE OF $1	TABLE 12-3 PRESENT VALUE OF $1	TABLE 13-1 AMOUNT OF ANNUITY OF $1	TABLE 13-2 PRESENT VALUE OF ANNUITY OF $1	TABLE 13-3 SINKING FUND VALUE OF $1
1	1.0950	0.9132	1.0000	0.9132	1.0000
2	1.1990	0.8340	2.0950	1.7473	0.4773
3	1.3129	0.7617	3.2940	2.5089	0.3036
4	1.4377	0.6956	4.6070	3.2045	0.2171
5	1.5742	0.6352	6.0446	3.8397	0.1654
6	1.7238	0.5801	7.6189	4.4198	0.1313
7	1.8876	0.5298	9.3427	4.9496	0.1070
8	2.0669	0.4838	11.2302	5.4334	0.0890
9	2.2632	0.4418	13.2971	5.8753	0.0752
10	2.4782	0.4035	15.5603	6.2788	0.0643
11	2.7137	0.3685	18.0385	6.6473	0.0554
12	2.9715	0.3365	20.7522	6.9838	0.0482
13	3.2537	0.3073	23.7236	7.2912	0.0422
14	3.5629	0.2807	26.9774	7.5719	0.0371
15	3.9013	0.2563	30.5402	7.8282	0.0327
16	4.2719	0.2341	34.4416	8.0623	0.0290
17	4.6778	0.2138	38.7135	8.2760	0.0258
18	5.1222	0.1952	43.3913	8.4713	0.0230
19	5.6088	0.1783	48.5135	8.6496	0.0206
20	6.1416	0.1628	54.1223	8.8124	0.0185
21	6.7251	0.1487	60.2639	8.9611	0.0166
22	7.3639	0.1358	66.9889	9.0969	0.0149
23	8.0635	0.1240	74.3529	9.2209	0.0134
24	8.8296	0.1133	82.4164	9.3341	0.0121
25	9.6684	0.1034	91.2460	9.4376	0.0110
26	10.5869	0.0945	100.9143	9.5320	0.0099
27	11.5926	0.0863	111.5012	9.6183	0.0090
28	12.6939	0.0788	123.0938	9.6971	0.0081
29	13.8998	0.0719	135.7877	9.7690	0.0074
30	15.2203	0.0657	149.6876	9.8347	0.0067
31	16.6663	0.0600	164.9079	9.8947	0.0061
32	18.2495	0.0548	181.5741	9.9495	0.0055
33	19.9833	0.0500	199.8237	9.9996	0.0050
34	21.8817	0.0457	219.8069	10.0453	0.0045
35	23.9604	0.0417	241.6886	10.0870	0.0041
36	26.2367	0.0381	265.6490	10.1251	0.0038
37	28.7291	0.0348	291.8857	10.1599	0.0034
38	31.4584	0.0318	320.6148	10.1917	0.0031
39	34.4470	0.0290	352.0732	10.2207	0.0028
40	37.7194	0.0265	386.5202	10.2472	0.0026
41	41.3028	0.0242	424.2396	10.2715	0.0024
42	45.2265	0.0221	465.5424	10.2936	0.0021
43	49.5231	0.0202	510.7689	10.3138	0.0020
44	54.2277	0.0184	560.2920	10.3322	0.0018
45	59.3794	0.0168	614.5197	10.3490	0.0016
46	65.0204	0.0154	673.8991	10.3644	0.0015
47	71.1974	0.0140	738.9195	10.3785	0.0014
48	77.9611	0.0128	810.1168	10.3913	0.0012
49	85.3674	0.0117	888.0779	10.4030	0.0011
50	93.4773	0.0107	973.4453	10.4137	0.0010

10%

PERIOD	TABLE 12-1 COMPOUND VALUE OF $1	TABLE 12-3 PRESENT VALUE OF $1	TABLE 13-1 AMOUNT OF ANNUITY OF $1	TABLE 13-2 PRESENT VALUE OF ANNUITY OF $1	TABLE 13-3 SINKING FUND VALUE OF $1
1	1.1000	0.9091	1.0000	0.9091	1.0000
2	1.2100	0.8264	2.1000	1.7355	0.4762
3	1.3310	0.7513	3.3100	2.4869	0.3021
4	1.4641	0.6830	4.6410	3.1699	0.2155
5	1.6105	0.6209	6.1051	3.7908	0.1638
6	1.7716	0.5645	7.7156	4.3553	0.1296
7	1.9487	0.5132	9.4872	4.8684	0.1054
8	2.1436	0.4665	11.4359	5.3349	0.0874
9	2.3579	0.4241	13.5795	5.7590	0.0736
10	2.5937	0.3855	15.9374	6.1446	0.0627
11	2.8531	0.3505	18.5312	6.4951	0.0540
12	3.1384	0.3186	21.3843	6.8137	0.0468
13	3.4523	0.2897	24.5227	7.1034	0.0408
14	3.7975	0.2633	27.9750	7.3667	0.0357
15	4.1772	0.2394	31.7725	7.6061	0.0315
16	4.5950	0.2176	35.9497	7.8237	0.0278
17	5.0545	0.1978	40.5447	8.0216	0.0247
18	5.5599	0.1799	45.5992	8.2014	0.0219
19	6.1159	0.1635	51.1591	8.3649	0.0195
20	6.7275	0.1486	57.2750	8.5136	0.0175
21	7.4002	0.1351	64.0025	8.6487	0.0156
22	8.1403	0.1228	71.4028	8.7715	0.0140
23	8.9543	0.1117	79.5430	8.8832	0.0126
24	9.8497	0.1015	88.4974	8.9847	0.0113
25	10.8347	0.0923	98.3471	9.0770	0.0102
26	11.9182	0.0839	109.1818	9.1609	0.0092
27	13.1100	0.0763	121.1000	9.2372	0.0083
28	14.4210	0.0693	134.2100	9.3066	0.0075
29	15.8631	0.0630	148.6310	9.3696	0.0067
30	17.4494	0.0573	164.4941	9.4269	0.0061
31	19.1944	0.0521	181.9435	9.4790	0.0055
32	21.1138	0.0474	201.1379	9.5264	0.0050
33	23.2252	0.0431	222.2517	9.5694	0.0045
34	25.5477	0.0391	245.4768	9.6086	0.0041
35	28.1025	0.0356	271.0245	9.6442	0.0037
36	30.9127	0.0323	299.1270	9.6765	0.0033
37	34.0040	0.0294	330.0397	9.7059	0.0030
38	37.4044	0.0267	364.0436	9.7327	0.0027
39	41.1448	0.0243	401.4480	9.7570	0.0025
40	45.2593	0.0221	442.5928	9.7790	0.0023
41	49.7852	0.0201	487.8520	9.7991	0.0020
42	54.7637	0.0183	537.6373	9.8174	0.0019
43	60.2401	0.0166	592.4010	9.8340	0.0017
44	66.2641	0.0151	652.6411	9.8491	0.0015
45	72.8905	0.0137	718.9052	9.8628	0.0014
46	80.1796	0.0125	791.7957	9.8753	0.0013
47	88.1975	0.0113	871.9753	9.8866	0.0011
48	97.0173	0.0103	960.1730	9.8969	0.0010
49	106.7190	0.0094	1057.1900	9.9063	0.0009
50	117.3909	0.0085	1163.9090	9.9148	0.0009

10½%

PERIOD	TABLE 12-1 COMPOUND VALUE OF $1	TABLE 12-3 PRESENT VALUE OF $1	TABLE 13-1 AMOUNT OF ANNUITY OF $1	TABLE 13-2 PRESENT VALUE OF ANNUITY OF $1	TABLE 13-3 SINKING FUND VALUE OF $1
1	1.1050	0.9050	1.0000	0.9050	1.0000
2	1.2210	0.8190	2.1050	1.7240	0.4751
3	1.3492	0.7412	3.3260	2.4651	0.3007
4	1.4909	0.6707	4.6753	3.1359	0.2139
5	1.6474	0.6070	6.1662	3.7429	0.1622
6	1.8204	0.5493	7.8136	4.2922	0.1280
7	2.0116	0.4971	9.6340	4.7893	0.1038
8	2.2228	0.4499	11.6456	5.2392	0.0859
9	2.4562	0.4071	13.8684	5.6463	0.0721
10	2.7141	0.3684	16.3246	6.0148	0.0613
11	2.9991	0.3334	19.0387	6.3482	0.0525
12	3.3140	0.3018	22.0377	6.6500	0.0454
13	3.6619	0.2731	25.3517	6.9230	0.0394
14	4.0464	0.2471	29.0136	7.1702	0.0345
15	4.4713	0.2236	33.0600	7.3938	0.0302
16	4.9408	0.2024	37.5313	7.5962	0.0266
17	5.4596	0.1832	42.4721	7.7794	0.0235
18	6.0328	0.1658	47.9317	7.9451	0.0209
19	6.6663	0.1500	53.9645	8.0952	0.0185
20	7.3662	0.1358	60.6308	8.2309	0.0165
21	8.1397	0.1229	67.9970	8.3538	0.0147
22	8.9944	0.1112	76.1367	8.4649	0.0131
23	9.9388	0.1006	85.1311	8.5656	0.0117
24	10.9823	0.0911	95.0699	8.6566	0.0105
25	12.1355	0.0824	106.0522	8.7390	0.0094
26	13.4097	0.0746	118.1877	8.8136	0.0085
27	14.8177	0.0675	131.5974	8.8811	0.0076
28	16.3736	0.0611	146.4151	8.9422	0.0068
29	18.0928	0.0553	162.7887	8.9974	0.0061
30	19.9926	0.0500	180.8815	9.0474	0.0055
31	22.0918	0.0453	200.8741	9.0927	0.0050
32	24.4114	0.0410	222.9659	9.1337	0.0045
33	26.9746	0.0371	247.3773	9.1707	0.0040
34	29.8070	0.0335	274.3519	9.2043	0.0036
35	32.9367	0.0304	304.1588	9.2347	0.0033
36	36.3950	0.0275	337.0955	9.2621	0.0030
37	40.2165	0.0249	373.4906	9.2870	0.0027
38	44.4392	0.0225	413.7070	9.3095	0.0024
39	49.1054	0.0204	458.1463	9.3299	0.0022
40	54.2614	0.0184	507.2517	9.3483	0.0020
41	59.9589	0.0167	561.5131	9.3650	0.0018
42	66.2546	0.0151	621.4720	9.3801	0.0016
43	73.2113	0.0137	687.7266	9.3937	0.0015
44	80.8985	0.0124	760.9378	9.4061	0.0013
45	89.3928	0.0112	841.8363	9.4173	0.0012
46	98.7791	0.0101	931.2291	9.4274	0.0011
47	109.1509	0.0092	1030.0080	9.4366	0.0010
48	120.6117	0.0083	1139.1590	9.4448	0.0009
49	133.2759	0.0075	1259.7710	9.4523	0.0008
50	147.2699	0.0068	1393.0470	9.4591	0.0007

11%

PERIOD	TABLE 12-1 COMPOUND VALUE OF $1	TABLE 12-3 PRESENT VALUE OF $1	TABLE 13-1 AMOUNT OF ANNUITY OF $1	TABLE 13-2 PRESENT VALUE OF ANNUITY OF $1	TABLE 13-3 SINKING FUND VALUE OF $1
1	1.1100	0.9009	1.0000	0.9009	1.0000
2	1.2321	0.8116	2.1100	1.7125	0.4739
3	1.3676	0.7312	3.3421	2.4437	0.2992
4	1.5181	0.6587	4.7097	3.1024	0.2123
5	1.6851	0.5935	6.2278	3.6959	0.1606
6	1.8704	0.5346	7.9129	4.2305	0.1264
7	2.0762	0.4817	9.7833	4.7122	0.1022
8	2.3045	0.4339	11.8594	5.1461	0.0843
9	2.5580	0.3909	14.1640	5.5370	0.0706
10	2.8394	0.3522	16.7220	5.8892	0.0598
11	3.1518	0.3173	19.5614	6.2065	0.0511
12	3.4985	0.2858	22.7132	6.4924	0.0440
13	3.8833	0.2575	26.2116	6.7499	0.0382
14	4.3104	0.2320	30.0949	6.9819	0.0332
15	4.7846	0.2090	34.4054	7.1909	0.0291
16	5.3109	0.1883	39.1899	7.3792	0.0255
17	5.8951	0.1696	44.5008	7.5488	0.0225
18	6.5436	0.1528	50.3959	7.7016	0.0198
19	7.2633	0.1377	56.9395	7.8393	0.0176
20	8.0623	0.1240	64.2028	7.9633	0.0156
21	8.9492	0.1117	72.2651	8.0751	0.0138
22	9.9336	0.1007	81.2143	8.1757	0.0123
23	11.0263	0.0907	91.1479	8.2664	0.0110
24	12.2392	0.0817	102.1741	8.3481	0.0098
25	13.5855	0.0736	114.4133	8.4217	0.0087
26	15.0799	0.0663	127.9988	8.4881	0.0078
27	16.7386	0.0597	143.0786	8.5478	0.0070
28	18.5799	0.0538	159.8173	8.6016	0.0063
29	20.6237	0.0485	178.3972	8.6501	0.0056
30	22.8923	0.0437	199.0209	8.6938	0.0050
31	25.4105	0.0394	221.9132	8.7331	0.0045
32	28.2056	0.0355	247.3236	8.7686	0.0040
33	31.3082	0.0319	275.5292	8.8005	0.0036
34	34.7521	0.0288	306.8374	8.8293	0.0033
35	38.5749	0.0259	341.5895	8.8552	0.0029
36	42.8181	0.0234	380.1644	8.8786	0.0026
37	47.5281	0.0210	422.9825	8.8996	0.0024
38	52.7562	0.0190	470.5106	8.9186	0.0021
39	58.5593	0.0171	523.2667	8.9357	0.0019
40	65.0009	0.0154	581.8260	8.9511	0.0017
41	72.1510	0.0139	646.8269	8.9649	0.0015
42	80.0876	0.0125	718.9779	8.9774	0.0014
43	88.8972	0.0112	799.0655	8.9886	0.0013
44	98.6759	0.0101	887.9626	8.9988	0.0011
45	109.5303	0.0091	986.6385	9.0079	0.0010
46	121.5786	0.0082	1096.1690	9.0161	0.0009
47	134.9522	0.0074	1217.7470	9.0235	0.0008
48	149.7970	0.0067	1352.7000	9.0302	0.0007
49	166.2746	0.0060	1502.4970	9.0362	0.0007
50	184.5649	0.0054	1668.7710	9.0417	0.0006

PERIOD	TABLE 12-1 COMPOUND VALUE OF $1	TABLE 12-3 PRESENT VALUE OF $1	TABLE 13-1 AMOUNT OF ANNUITY OF $1	TABLE 13-2 PRESENT VALUE OF ANNUITY OF $1	TABLE 13-3 SINKING FUND VALUE OF $1
1	1.1150	0.8969	1.0000	0.8969	1.0000
2	1.2432	0.8044	2.1150	1.7012	0.4728
3	1.3862	0.7214	3.3582	2.4226	0.2978
4	1.5456	0.6470	4.7444	3.0696	0.2108
5	1.7234	0.5803	6.2900	3.6499	0.1590
6	1.9215	0.5204	8.0134	4.1703	0.1248
7	2.1425	0.4667	9.9349	4.6370	0.1007
8	2.3889	0.4186	12.0774	5.0556	0.0828
9	2.6636	0.3754	14.4663	5.4311	0.0691
10	2.9699	0.3367	17.1300	5.7678	0.0584
11	3.3115	0.3020	20.0999	6.0697	0.0498
12	3.6923	0.2708	23.4114	6.3406	0.0427
13	4.1169	0.2429	27.1037	6.5835	0.0369
14	4.5904	0.2178	31.2206	6.8013	0.0320
15	5.1183	0.1954	35.8110	6.9967	0.0279
16	5.7069	0.1752	40.9293	7.1719	0.0244
17	6.3632	0.1572	46.6361	7.3291	0.0214
18	7.0949	0.1409	52.9993	7.4700	0.0189
19	7.9108	0.1264	60.0942	7.5964	0.0166
20	8.8206	0.1134	68.0050	7.7098	0.0147
21	9.8349	0.1017	76.8256	7.8115	0.0130
22	10.9660	0.0912	86.6606	7.9027	0.0115
23	12.2271	0.0818	97.6265	7.9845	0.0102
24	13.6332	0.0734	109.8536	8.0578	0.0091
25	15.2010	0.0658	123.4867	8.1236	0.0081
26	16.9491	0.0590	138.6877	8.1826	0.0072
27	18.8982	0.0529	155.6368	8.2355	0.0064
28	21.0715	0.0475	174.5350	8.2830	0.0057
29	23.4948	0.0426	195.6066	8.3255	0.0051
30	26.1967	0.0382	219.1013	8.3637	0.0046
31	29.2093	0.0342	245.2980	8.3979	0.0041
32	32.5683	0.0307	274.5072	8.4287	0.0036
33	36.3137	0.0275	307.0755	8.4562	0.0033
34	40.4898	0.0247	343.3892	8.4809	0.0029
35	45.1461	0.0222	383.8790	8.5030	0.0026
36	50.3379	0.0199	429.0250	8.5229	0.0023
37	56.1267	0.0178	479.3629	8.5407	0.0021
38	62.5813	0.0160	535.4896	8.5567	0.0019
39	69.7782	0.0143	598.0710	8.5710	0.0017
40	77.8027	0.0129	667.8491	8.5839	0.0015
41	86.7500	0.0115	745.6517	8.5954	0.0013
42	96.7262	0.0103	832.4017	8.6058	0.0012
43	107.8497	0.0093	929.1278	8.6150	0.0011
44	120.2524	0.0083	1036.9770	8.6233	0.0010
45	134.0815	0.0075	1157.2300	8.6308	0.0009
46	149.5008	0.0067	1291.3110	8.6375	0.0008
47	166.6934	0.0060	1440.8120	8.6435	0.0007
48	185.8632	0.0054	1607.5050	8.6489	0.0006
49	207.2374	0.0048	1793.3690	8.6537	0.0006
50	231.0697	0.0043	2000.6060	8.6580	0.0005

12%

PERIOD	TABLE 12-1 COMPOUND VALUE OF $1	TABLE 12-3 PRESENT VALUE OF $1	TABLE 13-1 AMOUNT OF ANNUITY OF $1	TABLE 13-2 PRESENT VALUE OF ANNUITY OF $1	TABLE 13-3 SINKING FUND VALUE OF $1
1	1.1200	0.8929	1.0000	0.8929	1.0000
2	1.2544	0.7972	2.1200	1.6901	0.4717
3	1.4049	0.7118	3.3744	2.4018	0.2963
4	1.5735	0.6355	4.7793	3.0373	0.2092
5	1.7623	0.5674	6.3528	3.6048	0.1574
6	1.9738	0.5066	8.1152	4.1114	0.1232
7	2.2107	0.4523	10.0890	4.5638	0.0991
8	2.4760	0.4039	12.2997	4.9676	0.0813
9	2.7731	0.3606	14.7757	5.3282	0.0677
10	3.1058	0.3220	17.5487	5.6502	0.0570
11	3.4785	0.2875	20.6546	5.9377	0.0484
12	3.8960	0.2567	24.1331	6.1944	0.0414
13	4.3635	0.2292	28.0291	6.4235	0.0357
14	4.8871	0.2046	32.3926	6.6282	0.0309
15	5.4736	0.1827	37.2797	6.8109	0.0268
16	6.1304	0.1631	42.7533	6.9740	0.0234
17	6.8660	0.1456	48.8837	7.1196	0.0205
18	7.6900	0.1300	55.7497	7.2497	0.0179
19	8.6128	0.1161	63.4397	7.3658	0.0158
20	9.6463	0.1037	72.0524	7.4694	0.0139
21	10.8038	0.0926	81.6987	7.5620	0.0122
22	12.1003	0.0826	92.5026	7.6446	0.0108
23	13.5523	0.0738	104.6029	7.7184	0.0096
24	15.1786	0.0659	118.1552	7.7843	0.0085
25	17.0001	0.0588	133.3338	7.8431	0.0075
26	19.0401	0.0525	150.3339	7.8957	0.0067
27	21.3249	0.0469	169.3740	7.9426	0.0059
28	23.8839	0.0419	190.6989	7.9844	0.0052
29	26.7499	0.0374	214.5827	8.0218	0.0047
30	29.9599	0.0334	241.3327	8.0552	0.0041
31	33.5551	0.0298	271.2926	8.0850	0.0037
32	37.5817	0.0266	304.8477	8.1116	0.0033
33	42.0915	0.0238	342.4294	8.1354	0.0029
34	47.1425	0.0212	384.5209	8.1566	0.0026
35	52.7996	0.0189	431.6634	8.1755	0.0023
36	59.1356	0.0169	484.4631	8.1924	0.0021
37	66.2318	0.0151	543.5986	8.2075	0.0018
38	74.1797	0.0135	609.8305	8.2210	0.0016
39	83.0812	0.0120	684.0101	8.2330	0.0015
40	93.0510	0.0107	767.0913	8.2438	0.0013
41	104.2171	0.0096	860.1422	8.2534	0.0012
42	116.7231	0.0086	964.3592	8.2619	0.0010
43	130.7299	0.0076	1081.0820	8.2696	0.0009
44	146.4175	0.0068	1211.8120	8.2764	0.0008
45	163.9876	0.0061	1358.2300	8.2825	0.0007
46	183.6661	0.0054	1522.2170	8.2880	0.0007
47	205.7060	0.0049	1705.8830	8.2928	0.0006
48	230.3908	0.0043	1911.5890	8.2972	0.0005
49	258.0377	0.0039	2141.9800	8.3010	0.0005
50	289.0022	0.0035	2400.0180	8.3045	0.0004

12½%

PERIOD	TABLE 12-1 COMPOUND VALUE OF $1	TABLE 12-3 PRESENT VALUE OF $1	TABLE 13-1 AMOUNT OF ANNUITY OF $1	TABLE 13-2 PRESENT VALUE OF ANNUITY OF $1	TABLE 13-3 SINKING FUND VALUE OF $1
1	1.1250	0.8889	1.0000	0.8889	1.0000
2	1.2656	0.7901	2.1250	1.6790	0.4706
3	1.4238	0.7023	3.3906	2.3813	0.2949
4	1.6018	0.6243	4.8145	3.0056	0.2077
5	1.8020	0.5549	6.4163	3.5606	0.1559
6	2.0273	0.4933	8.2183	4.0538	0.1217
7	2.2807	0.4385	10.2456	4.4923	0.0976
8	2.5658	0.3897	12.5263	4.8820	0.0798
9	2.8865	0.3464	15.0921	5.2285	0.0663
10	3.2473	0.3079	17.9786	5.5364	0.0556
11	3.6532	0.2737	21.2259	5.8102	0.0471
12	4.1099	0.2433	24.8791	6.0535	0.0402
13	4.6236	0.2163	28.9890	6.2698	0.0345
14	5.2016	0.1922	33.6126	6.4620	0.0298
15	5.8518	0.1709	38.8142	6.6329	0.0258
16	6.5833	0.1519	44.6660	6.7848	0.0224
17	7.4062	0.1350	51.2492	6.9198	0.0195
18	8.3319	0.1200	58.6554	7.0398	0.0170
19	9.3734	0.1067	66.9873	7.1465	0.0149
20	10.5451	0.0948	76.3607	7.2414	0.0131
21	11.8632	0.0843	86.9058	7.3256	0.0115
22	13.3461	0.0749	98.7691	7.4006	0.0101
23	15.0144	0.0666	112.1152	7.4672	0.0089
24	16.8912	0.0592	127.1296	7.5264	0.0079
25	19.0026	0.0526	144.0208	7.5790	0.0069
26	21.3779	0.0468	163.0234	7.6258	0.0061
27	24.0502	0.0416	184.4013	7.6674	0.0054
28	27.0564	0.0370	208.4515	7.7043	0.0048
29	30.4385	0.0329	235.5079	7.7372	0.0042
30	34.2433	0.0292	265.9464	7.7664	0.0038
31	38.5237	0.0260	300.1897	7.7923	0.0033
32	43.3392	0.0231	338.7134	7.8154	0.0030
33	48.7566	0.0205	382.0526	7.8359	0.0026
34	54.8512	0.0182	430.8092	7.8542	0.0023
35	61.7075	0.0162	485.6603	7.8704	0.0021
36	69.4210	0.0144	547.3679	7.8848	0.0018
37	78.0986	0.0128	616.7888	7.8976	0.0016
38	87.8609	0.0114	694.8874	7.9089	0.0014
39	98.8436	0.0101	782.7483	7.9191	0.0013
40	111.1990	0.0090	881.5918	7.9281	0.0011
41	125.0989	0.0080	992.7908	7.9360	0.0010
42	140.7362	0.0071	1117.8900	7.9432	0.0009
43	158.3283	0.0063	1258.6260	7.9495	0.0008
44	178.1193	0.0056	1416.9540	7.9551	0.0007
45	200.3842	0.0050	1595.0730	7.9601	0.0006
46	225.4322	0.0044	1795.4580	7.9645	0.0006
47	253.6113	0.0039	2020.8900	7.9685	0.0005
48	285.3127	0.0035	2274.5010	7.9720	0.0004
49	320.9768	0.0031	2559.8140	7.9751	0.0004
50	361.0988	0.0028	2880.7900	7.9778	0.0003

25

13%

PERIOD	TABLE 12-1 COMPOUND VALUE OF $1	TABLE 12-3 PRESENT VALUE OF $1	TABLE 13-1 AMOUNT OF ANNUITY OF $1	TABLE 13-2 PRESENT VALUE OF ANNUITY OF $1	TABLE 13-3 SINKING FUND VALUE OF $1
1	1.1300	0.8850	1.0000	0.8850	1.0000
2	1.2769	0.7831	2.1300	1.6681	0.4695
3	1.4429	0.6931	3.4069	2.3612	0.2935
4	1.6305	0.6133	4.8498	2.9745	0.2062
5	1.8424	0.5428	6.4803	3.5172	0.1543
6	2.0820	0.4803	8.3227	3.9975	0.1202
7	2.3526	0.4251	10.4047	4.4226	0.0961
8	2.6584	0.3762	12.7573	4.7988	0.0784
9	3.0040	0.3329	15.4157	5.1317	0.0649
10	3.3946	0.2946	18.4197	5.4262	0.0543
11	3.8359	0.2607	21.8143	5.6869	0.0458
12	4.3345	0.2307	25.6502	5.9176	0.0390
13	4.8980	0.2042	29.9847	6.1218	0.0334
14	5.5348	0.1807	34.8827	6.3025	0.0287
15	6.2543	0.1599	40.4174	6.4624	0.0247
16	7.0673	0.1415	46.6717	6.6039	0.0214
17	7.9861	0.1252	53.7390	6.7291	0.0186
18	9.0243	0.1108	61.7251	6.8399	0.0162
19	10.1974	0.0981	70.7494	6.9380	0.0141
20	11.5231	0.0868	80.9468	7.0248	0.0124
21	13.0211	0.0768	92.4698	7.1015	0.0108
22	14.7138	0.0680	105.4909	7.1695	0.0095
23	16.6266	0.0601	120.2047	7.2297	0.0083
24	18.7881	0.0532	136.8313	7.2829	0.0073
25	21.2305	0.0471	155.6194	7.3300	0.0064
26	23.9905	0.0417	176.8499	7.3717	0.0057
27	27.1093	0.0369	200.8404	7.4086	0.0050
28	30.6335	0.0326	227.9497	7.4412	0.0044
29	34.6158	0.0289	258.5831	7.4701	0.0039
30	39.1159	0.0256	293.1989	7.4957	0.0034
31	44.2009	0.0226	332.3148	7.5183	0.0030
32	49.9470	0.0200	376.5156	7.5383	0.0027
33	56.4402	0.0177	426.4627	7.5560	0.0023
34	63.7774	0.0157	482.9028	7.5717	0.0021
35	72.0684	0.0139	546.6802	7.5856	0.0018
36	81.4373	0.0123	618.7486	7.5979	0.0016
37	92.0242	0.0109	700.1858	7.6087	0.0014
38	103.9873	0.0096	792.2100	7.6183	0.0013
39	117.5057	0.0085	896.1972	7.6268	0.0011
40	132.7814	0.0075	1013.7030	7.6344	0.0010
41	150.0430	0.0067	1146.4840	7.6410	0.0009
42	169.5485	0.0059	1296.5270	7.6469	0.0008
43	191.5899	0.0052	1466.0760	7.6522	0.0007
44	216.4965	0.0046	1657.6650	7.6568	0.0006
45	244.6410	0.0041	1874.1620	7.6609	0.0005
46	276.4444	0.0036	2118.8030	7.6645	0.0005
47	312.3822	0.0032	2395.2470	7.6677	0.0004
48	352.9918	0.0028	2707.6290	7.6705	0.0004
49	398.8807	0.0025	3060.6210	7.6730	0.0003
50	450.7352	0.0022	3459.5010	7.6752	0.0003

13½%

PERIOD	TABLE 12-1 COMPOUND VALUE OF $1	TABLE 12-3 PRESENT VALUE OF $1	TABLE 13-1 AMOUNT OF ANNUITY OF $1	TABLE 13-2 PRESENT VALUE OF ANNUITY OF $1	TABLE 13-3 SINKING FUND VALUE OF $1
1	1.1350	0.8811	1.0000	0.8811	1.0000
2	1.2882	0.7763	2.1350	1.6573	0.4684
3	1.4621	0.6839	3.4232	2.3413	0.2921
4	1.6595	0.6026	4.8854	2.9438	0.2047
5	1.8836	0.5309	6.5449	3.4747	0.1528
6	2.1378	0.4678	8.4284	3.9425	0.1186
7	2.4264	0.4121	10.5663	4.3546	0.0946
8	2.7540	0.3631	12.9927	4.7177	0.0770
9	3.1258	0.3199	15.7467	5.0377	0.0635
10	3.5478	0.2819	18.8726	5.3195	0.0530
11	4.0267	0.2483	22.4204	5.5679	0.0446
12	4.5704	0.2188	26.4471	5.7867	0.0378
13	5.1874	0.1928	31.0175	5.9794	0.0322
14	5.8876	0.1698	36.2048	6.1493	0.0276
15	6.6825	0.1496	42.0925	6.2989	0.0238
16	7.5846	0.1318	48.7749	6.4308	0.0205
17	8.6085	0.1162	56.3596	6.5469	0.0177
18	9.7707	0.1023	64.9681	6.6493	0.0154
19	11.0897	0.0902	74.7388	6.7395	0.0134
20	12.5868	0.0794	85.8285	6.8189	0.0117
21	14.2861	0.0700	98.4154	6.8889	0.0102
22	16.2147	0.0617	112.7014	6.9506	0.0089
23	18.4037	0.0543	128.9161	7.0049	0.0078
24	20.8882	0.0479	147.3198	7.0528	0.0068
25	23.7081	0.0422	168.2080	7.0950	0.0059
26	26.9087	0.0372	191.9160	7.1321	0.0052
27	30.5413	0.0327	218.8247	7.1649	0.0046
28	34.6644	0.0288	249.3660	7.1937	0.0040
29	39.3441	0.0254	284.0304	7.2191	0.0035
30	44.6556	0.0224	323.3745	7.2415	0.0031
31	50.6841	0.0197	368.0301	7.2613	0.0027
32	57.5264	0.0174	418.7141	7.2786	0.0024
33	65.2925	0.0153	476.2405	7.2940	0.0021
34	74.1070	0.0135	541.5330	7.3075	0.0018
35	84.1114	0.0119	615.6400	7.3193	0.0016
36	95.4664	0.0105	699.7513	7.3298	0.0014
37	108.3544	0.0092	795.2177	7.3390	0.0013
38	122.9822	0.0081	903.5720	7.3472	0.0011
39	139.5848	0.0072	1026.5540	7.3543	0.0010
40	158.4288	0.0063	1166.1390	7.3607	0.0009
41	179.8167	0.0056	1324.5680	7.3662	0.0008
42	204.0919	0.0049	1504.3840	7.3711	0.0007
43	231.6443	0.0043	1708.4760	7.3754	0.0006
44	262.9163	0.0038	1940.1210	7.3792	0.0005
45	298.4100	0.0034	2203.0370	7.3826	0.0005
46	338.6953	0.0030	2501.4470	7.3855	0.0004
47	384.4192	0.0026	2840.1420	7.3881	0.0004
48	436.3158	0.0023	3224.5610	7.3904	0.0003
49	495.2184	0.0020	3660.8770	7.3924	0.0003
50	562.0728	0.0018	4156.0950	7.3942	0.0002

14%

PERIOD	TABLE 12-1 COMPOUND VALUE OF $1	TABLE 12-3 PRESENT VALUE OF $1	TABLE 13-1 AMOUNT OF ANNUITY OF $1	TABLE 13-2 PRESENT VALUE OF ANNUITY OF $1	TABLE 13-3 SINKING FUND VALUE OF $1
1	1.1400	0.8772	1.0000	0.8772	1.0000
2	1.2996	0.7695	2.1400	1.6467	0.4673
3	1.4815	0.6750	3.4396	2.3216	0.2907
4	1.6890	0.5921	4.9211	2.9137	0.2032
5	1.9254	0.5194	6.6101	3.4331	0.1513
6	2.1950	0.4556	8.5355	3.8887	0.1172
7	2.5023	0.3996	10.7305	4.2883	0.0932
8	2.8526	0.3506	13.2328	4.6389	0.0756
9	3.2519	0.3075	16.0853	4.9464	0.0622
10	3.7072	0.2697	19.3373	5.2161	0.0517
11	4.2262	0.2366	23.0445	5.4527	0.0434
12	4.8179	0.2076	27.2708	5.6603	0.0367
13	5.4924	0.1821	32.0887	5.8424	0.0312
14	6.2613	0.1597	37.5811	6.0021	0.0266
15	7.1379	0.1401	43.8424	6.1422	0.0228
16	8.1373	0.1229	50.9804	6.2651	0.0196
17	9.2765	0.1078	59.1176	6.3729	0.0169
18	10.5752	0.0946	68.3941	6.4674	0.0146
19	12.0557	0.0829	78.9692	6.5504	0.0127
20	13.7435	0.0728	91.0249	6.6231	0.0110
21	15.6676	0.0638	104.7684	6.6870	0.0095
22	17.8610	0.0560	120.4360	6.7429	0.0083
23	20.3616	0.0491	138.2971	6.7921	0.0072
24	23.2122	0.0431	158.6587	6.8351	0.0063
25	26.4619	0.0378	181.8708	6.8729	0.0055
26	30.1666	0.0331	208.3328	6.9061	0.0048
27	34.3899	0.0291	238.4994	6.9352	0.0042
28	39.2045	0.0255	272.8893	6.9607	0.0037
29	44.6931	0.0224	312.0938	6.9830	0.0032
30	50.9502	0.0196	356.7869	7.0027	0.0028
31	58.0832	0.0172	407.7371	7.0199	0.0025
32	66.2148	0.0151	465.8203	7.0350	0.0021
33	75.4849	0.0132	532.0351	7.0482	0.0019
34	86.0528	0.0116	607.5200	7.0599	0.0016
35	98.1002	0.0102	693.5728	7.0700	0.0014
36	111.8342	0.0089	791.6730	7.0790	0.0013
37	127.4910	0.0078	903.5072	7.0868	0.0011
38	145.3398	0.0069	1030.9980	7.0937	0.0010
39	165.6873	0.0060	1176.3380	7.0997	0.0009
40	188.8836	0.0053	1342.0250	7.1050	0.0007
41	215.3273	0.0046	1530.9090	7.1097	0.0007
42	245.4731	0.0041	1746.2360	7.1138	0.0006
43	279.8393	0.0036	1991.7090	7.1173	0.0005
44	319.0168	0.0031	2271.5480	7.1205	0.0004
45	363.6792	0.0027	2590.5650	7.1232	0.0004
46	414.5943	0.0024	2954.2450	7.1256	0.0003
47	472.6374	0.0021	3368.8390	7.1277	0.0003
48	538.8066	0.0019	3841.4760	7.1296	0.0003
49	614.2396	0.0016	4380.2830	7.1312	0.0002
50	700.2331	0.0014	4994.5230	7.1327	0.0002

PERIOD	TABLE 12-1 COMPOUND VALUE OF $1	TABLE 12-3 PRESENT VALUE OF $1	TABLE 13-1 AMOUNT OF ANNUITY OF $1	TABLE 13-2 PRESENT VALUE OF ANNUITY OF $1	TABLE 13-3 SINKING FUND VALUE OF $1
1	1.1450	0.8734	1.0000	0.8734	1.0000
2	1.3110	0.7628	2.1450	1.6361	0.4662
3	1.5011	0.6662	3.4560	2.3023	0.2893
4	1.7188	0.5818	4.9571	2.8841	0.2017
5	1.9680	0.5081	6.6759	3.3922	0.1498
6	2.2534	0.4438	8.6439	3.8360	0.1157
7	2.5801	0.3876	10.8973	4.2236	0.0918
8	2.9542	0.3385	13.4774	4.5621	0.0742
9	3.3826	0.2956	16.4316	4.8577	0.0609
10	3.8731	0.2582	19.8142	5.1159	0.0505
11	4.4347	0.2255	23.6873	5.3414	0.0422
12	5.0777	0.1969	28.1220	5.5383	0.0356
13	5.8139	0.1720	33.1996	5.7103	0.0301
14	6.6570	0.1502	39.0136	5.8606	0.0256
15	7.6222	0.1312	45.6705	5.9918	0.0219
16	8.7275	0.1146	53.2928	6.1063	0.0188
17	9.9929	0.1001	62.0202	6.2064	0.0161
18	11.4419	0.0874	72.0131	6.2938	0.0139
19	13.1010	0.0763	83.4551	6.3701	0.0120
20	15.0006	0.0667	96.5560	6.4368	0.0104
21	17.1757	0.0582	111.5566	6.4950	0.0090
22	19.6662	0.0508	128.7324	6.5459	0.0078
23	22.5178	0.0444	148.3986	6.5903	0.0067
24	25.7829	0.0388	170.9163	6.6291	0.0059
25	29.5214	0.0339	196.6992	6.6629	0.0051
26	33.8020	0.0296	226.2205	6.6925	0.0044
27	38.7033	0.0258	260.0225	6.7184	0.0038
28	44.3152	0.0226	298.7258	6.7409	0.0033
29	50.7409	0.0197	343.0410	6.7606	0.0029
30	58.0984	0.0172	393.7819	6.7778	0.0025
31	66.5226	0.0150	451.8802	6.7929	0.0022
32	76.1684	0.0131	518.4028	6.8060	0.0019
33	87.2128	0.0115	594.5712	6.8175	0.0017
34	99.8587	0.0100	681.7840	6.8275	0.0015
35	114.3382	0.0087	781.6426	6.8362	0.0013
36	130.9172	0.0076	895.9808	6.8439	0.0011
37	149.9002	0.0067	1026.8980	6.8505	0.0010
38	171.6357	0.0058	1176.7980	6.8564	0.0008
39	196.5229	0.0051	1348.4340	6.8615	0.0007
40	225.0187	0.0044	1544.9560	6.8659	0.0006
41	257.6464	0.0039	1769.9750	6.8698	0.0006
42	295.0051	0.0034	2027.6220	6.8732	0.0005
43	337.7808	0.0030	2322.6270	6.8761	0.0004
44	386.7590	0.0026	2660.4070	6.8787	0.0004
45	442.8391	0.0023	3047.1660	6.8810	0.0003
46	507.0507	0.0020	3490.0050	6.8830	0.0003
47	580.5730	0.0017	3997.0550	6.8847	0.0003
48	664.7561	0.0015	4577.6280	6.8862	0.0002
49	761.1456	0.0013	5242.3840	6.8875	0.0002
50	871.5118	0.0011	6003.5300	6.8886	0.0002

15%

PERIOD	TABLE 12-1 COMPOUND VALUE OF $1	TABLE 12-3 PRESENT VALUE OF $1	TABLE 13-1 AMOUNT OF ANNUITY OF $1	TABLE 13-2 PRESENT VALUE OF ANNUITY OF $1	TABLE 13-3 SINKING FUND VALUE OF $1
1	1.1500	0.8696	1.0000	0.8696	1.0000
2	1.3225	0.7561	2.1500	1.6257	0.4651
3	1.5209	0.6575	3.4725	2.2832	0.2880
4	1.7490	0.5718	4.9934	2.8550	0.2003
5	2.0114	0.4972	6.7424	3.3522	0.1483
6	2.3131	0.4323	8.7537	3.7845	0.1142
7	2.6600	0.3759	11.0668	4.1604	0.0904
8	3.0590	0.3269	13.7268	4.4873	0.0729
9	3.5179	0.2843	16.7858	4.7716	0.0596
10	4.0456	0.2472	20.3037	5.0188	0.0493
11	4.6524	0.2149	24.3493	5.2337	0.0411
12	5.3503	0.1869	29.0017	5.4206	0.0345
13	6.1528	0.1625	34.3519	5.5831	0.0291
14	7.0757	0.1413	40.5047	5.7245	0.0247
15	8.1371	0.1229	47.5804	5.8474	0.0210
16	9.3576	0.1069	55.7175	5.9542	0.0179
17	10.7613	0.0929	65.0751	6.0472	0.0154
18	12.3755	0.0808	75.8364	6.1280	0.0132
19	14.2318	0.0703	88.2118	6.1982	0.0113
20	16.3665	0.0611	102.4436	6.2593	0.0098
21	18.8215	0.0531	118.8101	6.3125	0.0084
22	21.6447	0.0462	137.6317	6.3587	0.0073
23	24.8915	0.0402	159.2764	6.3988	0.0063
24	28.6252	0.0349	184.1679	6.4338	0.0054
25	32.9190	0.0304	212.7930	6.4641	0.0047
26	37.8568	0.0264	245.7120	6.4906	0.0041
27	43.5353	0.0230	283.5688	6.5135	0.0035
28	50.0656	0.0200	327.1041	6.5335	0.0031
29	57.5755	0.0174	377.1697	6.5509	0.0027
30	66.2118	0.0151	434.7452	6.5660	0.0023
31	76.1436	0.0131	500.9570	6.5791	0.0020
32	87.5651	0.0114	577.1005	6.5905	0.0017
33	100.6998	0.0099	664.6656	6.6005	0.0015
34	115.8048	0.0086	765.3654	6.6091	0.0013
35	133.1755	0.0075	881.1702	6.6166	0.0011
36	153.1519	0.0065	1014.3460	6.6231	0.0010
37	176.1246	0.0057	1167.4980	6.6288	0.0009
38	202.5433	0.0049	1343.6220	6.6338	0.0007
39	232.9248	0.0043	1546.1660	6.6380	0.0006
40	267.8636	0.0037	1779.0910	6.6418	0.0006
41	308.0431	0.0032	2046.9540	6.6450	0.0005
42	354.2496	0.0028	2354.9970	6.6478	0.0004
43	407.3870	0.0025	2709.2470	6.6503	0.0004
44	468.4951	0.0021	3116.6340	6.6524	0.0003
45	538.7693	0.0019	3585.1290	6.6543	0.0003
46	619.5847	0.0016	4123.8990	6.6559	0.0002
47	712.5224	0.0014	4743.4830	6.6573	0.0002
48	819.4008	0.0012	5456.0060	6.6585	0.0002
49	942.3109	0.0011	6275.4070	6.6596	0.0002
50	1083.6580	0.0009	7217.7170	6.6605	0.0001

COMMON FRACTION TO DECIMAL CONVERSIONS

Fraction	Decimal equivalent	Fraction	Decimal equivalent	Fraction	Decimal equivalent
$\frac{1}{2}$	.50	$\frac{5}{6}$	$.83\frac{1}{3}(.83\overline{3})$	$\frac{1}{16}$	$.06\frac{1}{4}(.0625)$
$\frac{1}{3}$	$.33\frac{1}{3}(.33\overline{3})$	$\frac{1}{7}$	$.14\frac{2}{7}(.143)$	$\frac{3}{16}$	$.18\frac{3}{4}(.1875)$
$\frac{2}{3}$	$.66\frac{2}{3}(.66\overline{6})$	$\frac{1}{8}$	$.12\frac{1}{2}(.125)$	$\frac{5}{16}$	$.31\frac{1}{4}(.3125)$
$\frac{1}{4}$	.25	$\frac{3}{8}$	$.37\frac{1}{2}(.375)$	$\frac{7}{16}$	$.43\frac{3}{4}(.4375)$
$\frac{3}{4}$	.75	$\frac{5}{8}$	$.62\frac{1}{2}(.625)$	$\frac{9}{16}$	$.56\frac{1}{4}(.5625)$
$\frac{1}{5}$	.20	$\frac{7}{8}$	$.87\frac{1}{2}(.875)$	$\frac{11}{16}$	$.68\frac{3}{4}(.6875)$
$\frac{2}{5}$	.40	$\frac{1}{9}$	$.11\overline{1}$	$\frac{13}{16}$	$.81\frac{1}{4}(.8125)$
$\frac{3}{5}$	.60	$\frac{1}{10}$	.10	$\frac{15}{16}$	$.93\frac{3}{4}(.9375)$
$\frac{4}{5}$	.80	$\frac{1}{12}$	$.08\frac{1}{3}(.08\overline{3})$	$\frac{1}{20}$	.05
$\frac{1}{6}$	$.16\frac{2}{3}(.16\overline{6})$	$\frac{1}{15}$	$.06\frac{2}{3}(.06\overline{6})$	$\frac{1}{25}$	.04

Currencies

1/3/2012

U.S.-dollar foreign-exchange rates in late New York trading

Country/currency	—Fri— in US$	—Fri— per US$	US$ vs, YTD chg (%)
Americas			
Argentina peso*	.2321	4.3089	8.6
Brazil real	.5360	1.8657	12.3
Canada dollar	.9794	1.0210	2.6
Chile peso	.001924	519.86	11.1
Colombia peso	.0005153	1940.50	1.1
Ecuador US dollar	1	1	unch
Mexico peso*	.0717	13.9461	13.1
Peru new sol	.3709	2.696	−3.9
Uruguay peso†	.05047	19.8130	1.9
Venezuela b. fuerte	.229885	4.3500	unch
Asia-Pacific			
Australian dollar	1.0208	.9796	0.3
1-mos forward	1.0170	.9832	0.2
3-mos forward	1.0107	.9894	0.1
6-mos forward	1.0024	.9976	−0.2
China yuan	.1583	6.3190	−4.3
Hong Kong dollar	.1288	7.7669	−0.1
India rupee	.01886	53.025	18.3
Indonesia rupiah	.0001107	9033	1.6
Japan yen	.013001	76.92	−5.2
1-mos forward	.013008	76.88	−5.5
3-mos forward	.013025	76.78	−5.6
6-mos forward	.013054	76.60	−5.6
Malaysia ringgit	.3147	3.1775	5.1
New Zealand dollar	.7776	1.2860	0.3
Pakistan rupee	.01113	89.845	4.9
Philippines peso	.0228	43.850	0.3
Singapore dollar	.7713	1.2965	1.1
South Korea won	.0008616	1160.60	5.6
Taiwan dollar	.03304	30.265	4.2
Thailand baht	.03165	31.600	7.3
Vietnam dong	.00004753	21038	8.2

Country/currency	—Fri— in US$	—Fri— per US$	US$ vs, YTD chg (%)
Europe			
Czech Rep. koruna	.05063	19.751	5.8
Denmark krone	.1743	5.7373	3.1
Euro area euro	1.2960	.7716	3.3
Hungary forint	.004113	243.14	17.7
Norway krone	.1673	5.9766	2.6
Poland zloty	.2901	3.4470	16.9
Russia ruble‡	.03110	32.150	5.2
Sweden krona	.1453	6.8800	2.6
Switzerland franc	1.0670	.9372	0.2
1-mos forward	1.0675	.9368	0.2
3-mos forward	1.0691	.9354	0.2
6-mos forward	1.0718	.9330	0.1
Turkey lira**	.5217	1.9170	23.5
UK pound	1.5542	.6434	0.4
1-mos forward	1.5537	.6436	0.4
3-mos forward	1.5528	.6440	0.4
6-mos forward	1.5513	.6446	0.4
Middle East/Africa			
Bahrain dinar	2.6520	.3771	unch
Egypt pound*	.1653	6.0498	6.3
Israel shekel	.2624	3.8110	7.8
Jordan dinar	1.4095	.7095	0.1
Kuwait dinar	3.5945	.2782	−1.3
Lebanon pound	.0006645	1504.95	0.4
Saudi Arabia riyal	.2666	3.7504	unch
South Africa rand	.1237	8.0873	22.2
UAE dirham	.2722	3.6731	unch

*Floating rate †Financial ‡Russian Central Bank rate
**Commercial rate

Source: ICAP plc.

REFERENCE TABLE OF MEASURES

Measures of length

12 inches = 1 foot	10 millimeters = 1 centimeter
3 feet = 1 yard	10 centimeters = 1 decimeter
1,760 yards = 1 mile	10 decimeters = 1 meter
5,280 feet = 1 mile	1,000 meters = 1 kilometer
	1 inch = 2.54 centimeters

Measures of weight

16 ounces = 1 pound	1,000 milligrams = 1 gram
2,000 pounds = ton	100 centigrams = 1 gram
	1,000 grams = 1 kilogram
	2.2 pounds are about 1 kilogram

Measures of volume (capacity)

8 fluid ounces = 1 cup	1 liter = 1 cubic decimeter
2 cups = 1 pint	1,000 milliliters (cubic centimeters) = 1 liter
2 pints = 1 quart	1,000 liters = 1 kiloliter (cubic meter)
4 quarts = 1 gallon	

Surface measures

144 square inches = 1 square foot	100 square centimeters = 1 square decimeter
9 square feet = 1 square yard	100 square decimeters = 1 square meter
43,560 square feet = 1 acre	
640 acres = 1 square mile	

Time

60 seconds = 1 minute	7 days = 1 week	10 years = 1 decade
60 minutes = 1 hour	365 days = 1 year	100 years = 1 century
24 hours = 1 day	366 days = 1 leap year	1,000 years = 1 millenium

Payroll Period	One Withholding Allowance
Weekly	$ 73.08
Biweekly	146.15
Semimonthly	158.33
Monthly	316.67
Quarterly	950.00
Semiannually	1,900.00
Annually	3,800.00
Daily or miscellaneous (each day of the payroll period)	14.62

TABLE 1—WEEKLY Payroll Period

(a) SINGLE person (including head of household)—

If the amount of wages (after subtracting withholding allowances) is:

The amount of income tax to withhold is:

Not over $41 . . . . $0

Over—	But not over—		of excess over—
$41	—$209	. . . $0.00 plus 10%	—$41
$209	—$721	. . . $16.80 plus 15%	—$209
$721	—$1,688	. . . $93.60 plus 25%	—$721
$1,688	—$3,477	. . . $335.35 plus 28%	—$1,688
$3,477	—$7,510	. . . $836.27 plus 33%	—$3,477
$7,510	. . . .	$2,167.16 plus 35%	—$7,510

(b) MARRIED person—

If the amount of wages (after subtracting withholding allowances) is:

The amount of income tax to withhold is:

Not over $156 . . . . $0

Over—	But not over—		of excess over—
$156	—$490	. . . $0.00 plus 10%	—$156
$490	—$1,515	. . . $33.40 plus 15%	—$490
$1,515	—$2,900	. . . $187.15 plus 25%	—$1,515
$2,900	—$4,338	. . . $533.40 plus 28%	—$2,900
$4,338	—$7,624	. . . $936.04 plus 33%	—$4,338
$7,624	. . . .	$2,020.42 plus 35%	—$7,624

TABLE 2—BIWEEKLY Payroll Period

(a) SINGLE person (including head of household)—

If the amount of wages (after subtracting withholding allowances) is:

The amount of income tax to withhold is:

Not over $83 . . . . $0

Over—	But not over—		of excess over—
$83	—$417	. . . $0.00 plus 10%	—$83
$417	—$1,442	. . . $33.40 plus 15%	—$417
$1,442	—$3,377	. . . $187.15 plus 25%	—$1,442
$3,377	—$6,954	. . . $670.90 plus 28%	—$3,377
$6,954	—$15,019	. . . $1,672.46 plus 33%	—$6,954
$15,019	. . . .	$4,333.91 plus 35%	—$15,019

(b) MARRIED person—

If the amount of wages (after subtracting withholding allowances) is:

The amount of income tax to withhold is:

Not over $312 . . . . $0

Over—	But not over—		of excess over—
$312	—$981	. . . $0.00 plus 10%	—$312
$981	—$3,031	. . . $66.90 plus 15%	—$981
$3,031	—$5,800	. . . $374.40 plus 25%	—$3,031
$5,800	—$8,675	. . . $1,066.65 plus 28%	—$5,800
$8,675	—$15,248	. . . $1,871.65 plus 33%	—$8,675
$15,248	. . . .	$4,040.74 plus 35%	—$15,248

TABLE 3—SEMIMONTHLY Payroll Period

(a) SINGLE person (including head of household)—

If the amount of wages (after subtracting withholding allowances) is:

The amount of income tax to withhold is:

Not over $90 . . . . $0

Over—	But not over—		of excess over—
$90	—$452	. . . $0.00 plus 10%	—$90
$452	—$1,563	. . . $36.20 plus 15%	—$452
$1,563	—$3,658	. . . $202.85 plus 25%	—$1,563
$3,658	—$7,533	. . . $726.60 plus 28%	—$3,658
$7,533	—$16,271	. . . $1,811.60 plus 33%	—$7,533
$16,271	. . . .	$4,695.14 plus 35%	—$16,271

(b) MARRIED person—

If the amount of wages (after subtracting withholding allowances) is:

The amount of income tax to withhold is:

Not over $338 . . . . $0

Over—	But not over—		of excess over—
$338	—$1,063	. . . $0.00 plus 10%	—$338
$1,063	—$3,283	. . . $72.50 plus 15%	—$1,063
$3,283	—$6,283	. . . $405.50 plus 25%	—$3,283
$6,283	—$9,398	. . . $1,155.50 plus 28%	—$6,283
$9,398	$16,519	. . . $2,027.70 plus 33%	—$9,398
$16,519	. . . .	$4,377.63 plus 35%	—$16,519

TABLE 4—MONTHLY Payroll Period

(a) SINGLE person (including head of household)—

If the amount of wages (after subtracting withholding allowances) is:

The amount of income tax to withhold is:

Not over $179 . . . . $0

Over—	But not over—		of excess over—
$179	—$904	. . . $0.00 plus 10%	—$179
$904	—$3,125	. . . $72.50 plus 15%	—$904
$3,125	—$7,317	. . . $405.65 plus 25%	—$3,125
$7,317	—$15,067	. . . $1,453.65 plus 28%	—$7,317
$15,067	—$32,542	. . . $3,623.65 plus 33%	—$15,067
$32,542	. . . .	$9,390.40 plus 35%	—$32,542

(b) MARRIED person—

If the amount of wages (after subtracting withholding allowances) is:

The amount of income tax to withhold is:

Not over $675 . . . . $0

Over—	But not over—		of excess over—
$675	—$2,125	. . . $0.00 plus 10%	—$675
$2,125	—$6,567	. . . $145.00 plus 15%	—$2,125
$6,567	—$12,567	. . . $811.30 plus 25%	—$6,567
$12,567	—$18,796	. . . $2,311.30 plus 28%	—$12,567
$18,796	—$33,038	. . . $4,055.42 plus 33%	—$18,796
$33,038	. . . .	$8,755.28 plus 35%	—$33,038

And the wages are—		And the number of withholding allowances claimed is—										
At least	But less than	0	1	2	3	4	5	6	7	8	9	10
		The amount of income tax to be withheld is—										
$ 600	$ 610	$ 76	$ 65	$ 54	$ 43	$ 32	$ 21	$ 13	$ 5	$ 0	$ 0	$ 0
610	620	78	67	56	45	34	23	14	6	0	0	0
620	630	79	68	57	46	35	24	15	7	0	0	0
630	640	81	70	59	48	37	26	16	8	1	0	0
640	650	82	71	60	49	38	27	17	9	2	0	0
650	660	84	73	62	51	40	29	18	10	3	0	0
660	670	85	74	63	52	41	30	19	11	4	0	0
670	680	87	76	65	54	43	32	21	12	5	0	0
680	690	88	77	66	55	44	33	22	13	6	0	0
690	700	90	79	68	57	46	35	24	14	7	0	0
700	710	91	80	69	58	47	36	25	15	8	1	0
710	720	93	82	71	60	49	38	27	16	9	2	0
720	730	95	83	72	61	50	39	28	17	10	3	0
730	740	97	85	74	63	52	41	30	19	11	4	0
740	750	100	86	75	64	53	42	31	20	12	5	0
750	760	102	88	77	66	55	44	33	22	13	6	0
760	770	105	89	78	67	56	45	34	23	14	7	0
770	780	107	91	80	69	58	47	36	25	15	8	0
780	790	110	92	81	70	59	48	37	26	16	9	1
790	800	112	94	83	72	61	50	39	28	17	10	2
800	810	115	96	84	73	62	51	40	29	18	11	3
810	820	117	99	86	75	64	53	42	31	20	12	4
820	830	120	101	87	76	65	54	43	32	21	13	5
830	840	122	104	89	78	67	56	45	34	23	14	6
840	850	125	106	90	79	68	57	46	35	24	15	7
850	860	127	109	92	81	70	59	48	37	26	16	8
860	870	130	111	93	82	71	60	49	38	27	17	9
870	880	132	114	96	84	73	62	51	40	29	18	10
880	890	135	116	98	85	74	63	52	41	30	20	11
890	900	137	119	101	87	76	65	54	43	32	21	12
900	910	140	121	103	88	77	66	55	44	33	23	13
910	920	142	124	106	90	79	68	57	46	35	24	14
920	930	145	126	108	91	80	69	58	47	36	26	15
930	940	147	129	111	93	82	71	60	49	38	27	16
940	950	150	131	113	95	83	72	61	50	39	29	18
950	960	152	134	116	97	85	74	63	52	41	30	19
960	970	155	136	118	100	86	75	64	53	42	32	21
970	980	157	139	121	102	88	77	66	55	44	33	22
980	990	160	141	123	105	89	78	67	56	45	35	24
990	1,000	162	144	126	107	91	80	69	58	47	36	25
1,000	1,010	165	146	128	110	92	81	70	59	48	38	27
1,010	1,020	167	149	131	112	94	83	72	61	50	39	28
1,020	1,030	170	151	133	115	96	84	73	62	51	41	30
1,030	1,040	172	154	136	117	99	86	75	64	53	42	31
1,040	1,050	175	156	138	120	101	87	76	65	54	44	33
1,050	1,060	177	159	141	122	104	89	78	67	56	45	34
1,060	1,070	180	161	143	125	106	90	79	68	57	47	36
1,070	1,080	182	164	146	127	109	92	81	70	59	48	37
1,080	1,090	185	166	148	130	111	93	82	71	60	50	39
1,090	1,100	187	169	151	132	114	96	84	73	62	51	40
1,100	1,110	190	171	153	135	116	98	85	74	63	53	42
1,110	1,120	192	174	156	137	119	101	87	76	65	54	43
1,120	1,130	195	176	158	140	121	103	88	77	66	56	45
1,130	1,140	197	179	161	142	124	106	90	79	68	57	46
1,140	1,150	200	181	163	145	126	108	91	80	69	59	48
1,150	1,160	202	184	166	147	129	111	93	82	71	60	49
1,160	1,170	205	186	168	150	131	113	95	83	72	62	51
1,170	1,180	207	189	171	152	134	116	97	85	74	63	52
1,180	1,190	210	191	173	155	136	118	100	86	75	65	54
1,190	1,200	212	194	176	157	139	121	102	88	77	66	55
1,200	1,210	215	196	178	160	141	123	105	89	78	68	57
1,210	1,220	217	199	181	162	144	126	107	91	80	69	58
1,220	1,230	220	201	183	165	146	128	110	92	81	71	60
1,230	1,240	222	204	186	167	149	131	112	94	83	72	61
1,240	1,250	225	206	188	170	151	133	115	97	84	74	63

And the wages are—		And the number of withholding allowances claimed is—										
At least	But less than	0	1	2	3	4	5	6	7	8	9	10
		The amount of income tax to be withheld is—										
$800	$810	$ 81	$ 70	$ 59	$ 48	$ 37	$ 28	$ 21	$ 14	$ 6	$ 0	$ 0
810	820	82	71	60	49	38	29	22	15	7	0	0
820	830	84	73	62	51	40	30	23	16	8	1	0
830	840	85	74	63	52	41	31	24	17	9	2	0
840	850	87	76	65	54	43	32	25	18	10	3	0
850	860	88	77	66	55	44	33	26	19	11	4	0
860	870	90	79	68	57	46	35	27	20	12	5	0
870	880	91	80	69	58	47	36	28	21	13	6	0
880	890	93	82	71	60	49	38	29	22	14	7	0
890	900	94	83	72	61	50	39	30	23	15	8	1
900	910	96	85	74	63	52	41	31	24	16	9	2
910	920	97	86	75	64	53	42	32	25	17	10	3
920	930	99	88	77	66	55	44	33	26	18	11	4
930	940	100	89	78	67	56	45	34	27	19	12	5
940	950	102	91	80	69	58	47	36	28	20	13	6
950	960	103	92	81	70	59	48	37	29	21	14	7
960	970	105	94	83	72	61	50	39	30	22	15	8
970	980	106	95	84	73	62	51	40	31	23	16	9
980	990	108	97	86	75	64	53	42	32	24	17	10
990	1,000	109	98	87	76	65	54	43	33	25	18	11
1,000	1,010	111	100	89	78	67	56	45	34	26	19	12
1,010	1,020	112	101	90	79	68	57	46	35	27	20	13
1,020	1,030	114	103	92	81	70	59	48	37	28	21	14
1,030	1,040	115	104	93	82	71	60	49	38	29	22	15
1,040	1,050	117	106	95	84	73	62	51	40	30	23	16
1,050	1,060	118	107	96	85	74	63	52	41	31	24	17
1,060	1,070	120	109	98	87	76	65	54	43	32	25	18
1,070	1,080	121	110	99	88	77	66	55	44	33	26	19
1,080	1,090	123	112	101	90	79	68	57	46	35	27	20
1,090	1,100	124	113	102	91	80	69	58	47	36	28	21
1,100	1,110	126	115	104	93	82	71	60	49	38	29	22
1,110	1,120	127	116	105	94	83	72	61	50	39	30	23
1,120	1,130	129	118	107	96	85	74	63	52	41	31	24
1,130	1,140	130	119	108	97	86	75	64	53	42	32	25
1,140	1,150	132	121	110	99	88	77	66	55	44	33	26
1,150	1,160	133	122	111	100	89	78	67	56	45	35	27
1,160	1,170	135	124	113	102	91	80	69	58	47	36	28
1,170	1,180	136	125	114	103	92	81	70	59	48	38	29
1,180	1,190	138	127	116	105	94	83	72	61	50	39	30
1,190	1,200	139	128	117	106	95	84	73	62	51	41	31
1,200	1,210	141	130	119	108	97	86	75	64	53	42	32
1,210	1,220	142	131	120	109	98	87	76	65	54	44	33
1,220	1,230	144	133	122	111	100	89	78	67	56	45	34
1,230	1,240	145	134	123	112	101	90	79	68	57	47	36
1,240	1,250	147	136	125	114	103	92	81	70	59	48	37
1,250	1,260	148	137	126	115	104	93	82	71	60	50	39
1,260	1,270	150	139	128	117	106	95	84	73	62	51	40
1,270	1,280	151	140	129	118	107	96	85	74	63	53	42
1,280	1,290	153	142	131	120	109	98	87	76	65	54	43
1,290	1,300	154	143	132	121	110	99	88	77	66	56	45
1,300	1,310	156	145	134	123	112	101	90	79	68	57	46
1,310	1,320	157	146	135	124	113	102	91	80	69	59	48
1,320	1,330	159	148	137	126	115	104	93	82	71	60	49
1,330	1,340	160	149	138	127	116	105	94	83	72	62	51
1,340	1,350	162	151	140	129	118	107	96	85	74	63	52
1,350	1,360	163	152	141	130	119	108	97	86	75	65	54
1,360	1,370	165	154	143	132	121	110	99	88	77	66	55
1,370	1,380	166	155	144	133	122	111	100	89	78	68	57
1,380	1,390	168	157	146	135	124	113	102	91	80	69	58
1,390	1,400	169	158	147	136	125	114	103	92	81	71	60

INTEREST ON A $1 DEPOSIT COMPOUNDED DAILY—360-DAY BASIS

Number of years	6.00%	6.50%	7.00%	7.50%	8.00%	8.50%	9.00%	9.50%	10.00%
1	1.0618	1.0672	1.0725	1.0779	1.0833	1.0887	1.0942	1.0996	1.1052
2	1.1275	1.1388	1.1503	1.1618	1.1735	1.1853	1.1972	1.2092	1.2214
3	1.1972	1.2153	1.2337	1.2523	1.2712	1.2904	1.3099	1.3297	1.3498
4	1.2712	1.2969	1.3231	1.3498	1.3771	1.4049	1.4333	1.4622	1.4917
5	1.3498	1.3840	1.4190	1.4549	1.4917	1.5295	1.5682	1.6079	1.6486
6	1.4333	1.4769	1.5219	1.5682	1.6160	1.6652	1.7159	1.7681	1.8220
7	1.5219	1.5761	1.6322	1.6904	1.7506	1.8129	1.8775	1.9443	2.0136
8	1.6160	1.6819	1.7506	1.8220	1.8963	1.9737	2.0543	2.1381	2.2253
9	1.7159	1.7949	1.8775	1.9639	2.0543	2.1488	2.2477	2.3511	2.4593
10	1.8220	1.9154	2.0136	2.1168	2.2253	2.3394	2.4593	2.5854	2.7179
15	2.4594	2.6509	2.8574	3.0799	3.3197	3.5782	3.8568	4.1571	4.4808
20	3.3198	3.6689	4.0546	4.4810	4.9522	5.4728	6.0482	6.6842	7.3870
25	4.4811	5.0777	5.7536	6.5195	7.3874	8.3708	9.4851	10.7477	12.1782
30	6.0487	7.0275	8.1645	9.4855	11.0202	12.8032	14.8747	17.2813	20.0772

THE TAX REFORM ACT UPDATE: ACCELERATED COST RECOVERY SYSTEM FOR ASSETS PLACED IN SERVICE AFTER DECEMBER 31, 1986*

The following classes use a 200% declining-balance, switching to straight-line:

3-year: Race horses more than two years old or any horse other than a race horse that is more than 12 years old at time placed into service; special tools of certain industries.

5-year: Automobiles (not luxury); taxis; light general-purpose trucks, semiconductor manufacturing equipment; computer-based telephone central office switching equipment; qualified technological equipment; property used in connection with research and experimentation.

7-year: Railroad track; single-purpose agricultural (pigpens) or horticultural structure; fixtures, equipment, and furniture.

10-year: New law doesn't add any specific property under this class.

The following classes use 150% declining-balance, switching to straight-line:

15-year: Municipal wastewater treatment plants; telephone distribution plants and comparable equipment for two-way exchange of voice and data communications.

20-year: Municipal sewers.

The following classes use straight-line:

27.5-year: Only residential rental property.
31.5-year: Only nonresidential real property.

*New tax bill of 1989 requires for cellular phones the straight-line depreciation unless 50% is for business use.

MACRS

Year of recovery	3-year	5-year	7-year	10-year	15-year	20-year
1	33%	20.00%	14.28%	10.00%	5.00%	3.75%
2	45%	32.00%	24.49%	18.00%	9.50%	7.22%
3	15%	19.20%	17.49%	14.40%	8.55%	6.68%
4	7%	11.52%	12.49%	11.52%	7.69%	6.18%
5		11.52%	8.93%	9.22%	6.93%	5.71%
6		5.76%	8.93%	7.37%	6.23%	5.28%
7			8.93%	6.55%	5.90%	4.89%
8			4.46%	6.55%	5.90%	4.52%
9				6.55%	5.90%	4.46%
10				6.55%	5.90%	4.46%
11				3.29%	5.90%	4.46%
12					5.90%	4.46%
13					5.90%	4.46%
14					5.90%	4.46%
15					5.90%	4.46%
16					3.00%	4.46%
17						4.46%
18						4.46%
19						4.46%
20						4.46%
21						2.25%

NUMBER OF PAYMENTS	2.00%	2.25%	2.50%	2.75%	3.00%	3.25%	3.50%	3.75%	4.00%	4.25%	4.50%	4.75%	5.00%	5.25%	5.50%	5.75%
						(FINANCE CHARGE PER $100 OF AMOUNT FINANCED)										
1	0.17	0.19	0.21	0.23	0.25	0.27	0.29	0.31	0.33	0.35	0.37	0.40	0.42	0.44	0.46	0.48
2	0.25	0.28	0.31	0.34	0.38	0.41	0.44	0.47	0.50	0.53	3.56	0.59	0.63	0.66	0.69	0.72
3	0.33	0.38	0.42	0.46	0.50	0.54	0.58	0.63	0.67	0.71	0.75	0.79	0.83	0.88	0.92	0.96
4	0.42	0.47	0.52	0.57	0.63	0.68	0.73	0.78	0.83	0.89	0.94	0.99	1.04	1.10	1.15	1.20
5	0.50	0.56	0.63	0.69	0.75	0.81	0.88	0.94	1.00	1.07	1.13	1.19	1.25	1.32	1.39	1.44
6	0.58	0.66	0.73	0.80	0.88	0.95	1.02	1.10	1.17	1.24	1.32	1.39	1.46	1.54	1.61	1.68
7	0.67	0.75	0.84	0.92	1.00	1.09	1.17	1.25	1.34	1.42	1.51	1.59	1.67	1.76	1.84	1.93
8	0.75	0.85	0.94	1.03	1.13	1.22	1.32	1.41	1.51	1.60	1.69	1.79	1.88	1.98	2.07	2.17
9	0.84	0.94	1.04	1.15	1.25	1.36	1.46	1.57	1.67	1.78	1.88	1.99	2.09	2.20	2.31	2.41
10	0.92	1.03	1.15	1.26	1.38	1.50	1.61	1.73	1.84	1.96	2.07	2.19	2.31	2.42	2.54	2.65
11	1.00	1.13	1.25	1.38	1.51	1.63	1.76	1.88	2.01	2.14	2.26	2.39	2.52	2.64	2.77	2.90
12	1.09	1.22	1.36	1.50	1.63	1.77	1.91	2.04	2.18	2.32	2.45	2.59	2.73	2.87	3.00	3.14
13	1.17	1.32	1.46	1.61	1.76	1.91	2.05	2.20	2.35	2.50	2.64	2.79	2.94	3.09	3.24	3.39
14	1.25	1.41	1.57	1.73	1.89	2.04	2.20	2.36	2.52	2.68	2.84	2.99	3.15	3.31	3.47	3.63
15	1.34	1.51	1.67	1.84	2.01	2.18	2.35	2.52	2.69	2.86	3.03	3.20	3.37	3.54	3.71	3.88
16	1.42	1.60	1.78	1.96	2.14	2.32	2.50	2.68	2.86	3.04	3.22	3.40	3.58	3.76	3.94	4.12
17	1.51	1.70	1.89	2.08	2.26	2.46	2.65	2.84	3.03	3.22	3.41	3.60	3.79	3.98	4.18	4.37
18	1.59	1.79	1.99	2.19	2.39	2.59	2.79	2.99	3.20	3.40	3.60	3.80	4.00	4.21	4.41	4.61
19	1.67	1.89	2.10	2.31	2.52	2.73	2.94	3.15	3.37	3.58	3.79	4.01	4.22	4.43	4.65	4.86
20	1.76	1.98	2.20	2.42	2.65	2.87	3.09	3.31	3.54	3.76	3.98	4.21	4.43	4.66	4.88	5.11
21	1.84	2.08	2.31	2.54	2.77	3.01	3.24	3.47	3.71	3.94	4.18	4.41	4.65	4.89	5.12	5.35
22	1.93	2.17	2.41	2.66	2.90	3.14	3.39	3.63	3.88	4.12	4.37	4.62	4.86	5.11	5.36	5.60
23	2.01	2.27	2.52	2.77	3.03	3.28	3.54	3.79	4.05	4.31	4.56	4.82	5.08	5.33	5.59	5.85
24	2.10	2.36	2.62	2.89	3.15	3.42	3.69	3.95	4.22	4.49	4.75	5.02	5.29	5.56	5.83	6.10
25	2.18	2.46	2.73	3.01	3.28	3.56	3.84	4.11	4.39	4.67	4.95	5.23	5.51	5.79	6.07	6.35
26	2.27	2.55	2.84	3.12	3.41	3.70	3.99	4.27	4.56	4.85	5.14	5.43	5.72	6.01	6.31	6.60
27	2.35	2.65	2.94	3.24	3.54	3.84	4.13	4.43	4.73	5.03	5.34	5.64	5.94	6.24	6.54	6.85
28	2.43	2.74	3.05	3.36	3.67	3.97	4.28	4.59	4.91	5.22	5.53	5.84	6.15	6.47	6.78	7.10
29	2.52	2.84	3.16	3.47	3.79	4.11	4.43	4.76	5.08	5.40	5.72	6.05	6.37	6.70	7.02	7.35
30	2.60	2.93	3.26	3.59	3.92	4.25	4.58	4.92	5.25	5.58	5.92	6.25	6.59	6.92	7.26	7.60
31	2.69	3.03	3.37	3.71	4.05	4.39	4.73	5.08	5.42	5.77	6.11	6.46	6.81	7.15	7.50	7.85
32	2.77	3.12	3.47	3.83	4.18	4.53	4.88	5.24	5.59	5.95	6.31	6.66	7.02	7.38	7.74	8.10
33	2.86	3.22	3.58	3.94	4.31	4.67	5.04	5.40	5.77	6.13	6.50	6.87	7.24	7.61	7.98	8.35
34	2.94	3.32	3.69	4.06	4.44	4.81	5.19	5.56	5.94	6.32	6.70	7.08	7.46	7.84	8.22	8.61
35	3.03	3.41	3.79	4.18	4.56	4.95	5.34	5.72	6.11	6.50	6.89	7.28	7.68	8.07	8.46	8.86
36	3.11	3.51	3.90	4.30	4.69	5.09	5.49	5.89	6.29	6.69	7.09	7.49	7.90	8.30	8.71	9.11
37	3.20	3.60	4.01	4.41	4.82	5.23	5.64	6.05	6.46	6.87	7.28	7.70	8.11	8.53	8.95	9.37
38	3.28	3.70	4.11	4.53	4.95	5.37	5.79	6.21	6.63	7.06	7.48	7.91	8.33	8.76	9.19	9.62
39	3.37	3.79	4.22	4.65	5.08	5.51	5.94	6.37	6.81	7.24	7.68	8.11	8.55	8.99	9.43	9.87
40	3.45	3.89	4.33	4.77	5.21	5.65	6.09	6.54	6.98	7.43	7.87	8.32	8.77	9.22	9.67	10.13
41	3.54	3.99	4.44	4.89	5.34	5.79	6.24	6.70	7.16	7.61	8.07	8.53	8.99	9.45	9.92	10.38
42	3.62	4.08	4.54	5.00	5.47	5.93	6.40	6.86	7.33	7.80	8.27	8.74	9.21	9.69	10.16	10.64
43	3.71	4.18	4.65	5.12	5.60	6.07	6.55	7.03	7.50	7.98	8.47	8.95	9.43	9.92	10.41	10.89
44	3.79	4.28	4.76	5.24	5.73	6.21	6.70	7.19	7.68	8.17	8.66	9.16	9.65	10.15	10.65	11.15
45	3.88	4.37	4.86	5.36	5.86	6.35	6.85	7.35	7.85	8.36	8.86	9.37	9.88	10.38	10.89	11.41
46	3.97	4.47	4.97	5.48	5.98	6.49	7.00	7.52	8.03	8.54	9.06	9.58	10.10	10.62	11.14	11.66
47	4.05	4.56	5.08	5.60	6.11	6.63	7.16	7.68	8.20	8.73	9.26	9.79	10.32	10.85	11.39	11.92
48	4.14	4.66	5.19	5.72	6.24	6.78	7.31	7.84	8.38	8.92	9.46	10.00	10.54	11.09	11.63	12.18
49	4.22	4.76	5.30	5.83	6.37	6.92	7.46	8.01	8.56	9.10	9.66	10.21	10.76	11.32	11.88	12.44
50	4.31	4.85	5.40	5.95	6.50	7.06	7.61	8.17	8.73	9.29	9.85	10.42	10.99	11.55	12.12	12.70
51	4.39	4.95	5.51	6.07	6.64	7.20	7.77	8.34	8.91	9.48	10.05	10.63	11.21	11.79	12.37	12.95
52	4.48	5.05	5.62	6.19	6.77	7.34	7.92	8.50	9.08	9.67	10.25	10.84	11.43	12.02	12.62	13.21
53	4.56	5.14	5.73	6.31	6.90	7.48	8.07	8.67	9.26	9.86	10.45	11.05	11.66	12.26	12.86	13.47
54	4.65	5.24	5.83	6.43	7.03	7.63	8.23	8.83	9.44	10.04	10.65	11.26	11.88	12.49	13.11	13.73
55	4.74	5.34	5.94	6.55	7.16	7.77	8.38	9.00	9.61	10.23	10.85	11.48	12.10	12.73	13.36	13.99
56	4.82	5.44	6.05	6.67	7.29	7.91	8.53	9.16	9.79	10.42	11.05	11.69	12.33	12.97	13.61	14.25
57	4.91	5.53	6.16	6.79	7.42	8.05	8.69	9.33	9.97	10.61	11.25	11.90	12.55	13.20	13.86	14.52
58	4.99	5.63	6.27	6.91	7.55	8.19	8.84	9.49	10.14	10.80	11.46	12.11	12.78	13.44	14.11	14.78
59	5.08	5.73	6.38	7.03	7.68	8.34	9.00	9.66	10.32	10.99	11.66	12.33	13.00	13.68	14.36	15.04
60	5.17	5.82	6.48	7.15	7.81	8.48	9.15	9.82	10.50	11.18	11.86	12.54	13.23	13.92	14.61	15.30

ANNUAL PERCENTAGE RATE

NUMBER OF PAYMENTS	6.00%	6.25%	6.50%	6.75%	7.00%	7.25%	7.50%	7.75%	8.00%	8.25%	8.50%	8.75%	9.00%	9.25%	9.50%	9.75%
					(FINANCE CHARGE PER $100 OF AMOUNT FINANCED)											
1	0.50	0.52	0.54	0.56	0.58	0.60	0.62	0.65	0.67	0.69	0.71	0.73	0.75	0.77	0.79	0.81
2	0.75	0.78	0.81	0.84	0.88	0.91	0.94	0.97	1.00	1.03	1.06	1.10	1.13	1.16	1.19	1.22
3	1.00	1.04	1.09	1.13	1.17	1.21	1.25	1.29	1.34	1.38	1.42	1.46	1.50	1.55	1.59	1.63
4	1.25	1.31	1.36	1.41	1.46	1.51	1.57	1.62	1.67	1.72	1.78	1.83	1.88	1.93	1.99	2.04
5	1.50	1.57	1.63	1.69	1.76	1.82	1.88	1.95	2.01	2.07	2.13	2.20	2.26	2.32	2.39	2.45
6	1.76	1.83	1.90	1.98	2.05	2.13	2.20	2.27	2.35	2.42	2.49	2.57	2.64	2.72	2.79	2.86
7	2.01	2.09	2.18	2.26	2.35	2.43	2.52	2.60	2.68	2.77	2.85	2.94	3.02	3.11	3.19	3.28
8	2.26	2.36	2.45	2.55	2.64	2.74	2.83	2.93	3.02	3.12	3.21	3.31	3.40	3.50	3.60	3.69
9	2.52	2.62	2.73	2.83	2.94	3.05	3.15	3.26	3.36	3.47	3.57	3.68	3.79	3.89	4.00	4.11
10	2.77	2.89	3.00	3.12	3.24	3.35	3.47	3.59	3.70	3.82	3.94	4.05	4.17	4.29	4.41	4.52
11	3.02	3.15	3.28	3.41	3.53	3.66	3.79	3.92	4.04	4.17	4.30	4.43	4.56	4.68	4.81	4.94
12	3.28	3.42	3.56	3.69	3.83	3.97	4.11	4.25	4.39	4.52	4.66	4.80	4.94	5.08	5.22	5.36
13	3.53	3.68	3.83	3.98	4.13	4.28	4.43	4.58	4.73	4.88	5.03	5.18	5.33	5.48	5.63	5.78
14	3.79	3.95	4.11	4.27	4.43	4.59	4.75	4.91	5.07	5.23	5.39	5.55	5.72	5.88	6.04	6.20
15	4.05	4.22	4.39	4.56	4.73	4.90	5.07	5.24	5.42	5.59	5.76	5.93	6.10	6.28	6.45	6.62
16	4.30	4.48	4.67	4.85	5.03	5.21	5.40	5.58	5.76	5.94	6.13	6.31	6.49	6.68	6.86	7.05
17	4.56	4.75	4.95	5.14	5.33	5.52	5.72	5.91	6.11	6.30	6.49	6.69	6.88	7.08	7.27	7.47
18	4.82	5.02	5.22	5.43	5.63	5.84	6.04	6.25	6.45	6.66	6.86	7.07	7.28	7.48	7.69	7.90
19	5.07	5.29	5.50	5.72	5.94	6.15	6.37	6.58	6.80	7.02	7.23	7.45	7.67	7.89	8.10	8.32
20	5.33	5.56	5.78	6.01	6.24	6.46	6.69	6.92	7.15	7.38	7.60	7.83	8.06	8.29	8.52	8.75
21	5.59	5.83	6.07	6.30	6.54	6.78	7.02	7.26	7.50	7.74	7.97	8.21	8.46	8.70	8.94	9.18
22	5.85	6.10	6.35	6.60	6.84	7.09	7.34	7.59	7.84	8.10	8.35	8.60	8.85	9.10	9.36	9.61
23	6.11	6.37	6.63	6.89	7.15	7.41	7.67	7.93	8.19	8.46	8.72	8.98	9.25	9.51	9.77	10.04
24	6.37	6.64	6.91	7.18	7.45	7.73	8.00	8.27	8.55	8.82	9.09	9.37	9.64	9.92	10.19	10.47
25	6.63	6.91	7.19	7.48	7.76	8.04	8.33	8.61	8.90	9.18	9.47	9.75	10.04	10.33	10.62	10.90
26	6.89	7.18	7.48	7.77	8.07	8.36	8.66	8.95	9.25	9.55	9.84	10.14	10.44	10.74	11.04	11.34
27	7.15	7.46	7.76	8.07	8.37	8.68	8.99	9.29	9.60	9.91	10.22	10.53	10.84	11.15	11.46	11.77
28	7.41	7.73	8.05	8.36	8.68	9.00	9.32	9.64	9.96	10.28	10.60	10.92	11.24	11.56	11.89	12.21
29	7.67	8.00	8.33	8.66	8.99	9.32	9.65	9.98	10.31	10.64	10.97	11.31	11.64	11.98	12.31	12.65
30	7.94	8.28	8.61	8.96	9.30	9.64	9.98	10.32	10.66	11.01	11.35	11.70	12.04	12.39	12.74	13.09
31	8.20	8.55	8.90	9.25	9.60	9.96	10.31	10.67	11.02	11.38	11.73	12.09	12.45	12.81	13.17	13.53
32	8.46	8.82	9.19	9.55	9.91	10.28	10.64	11.01	11.38	11.74	12.11	12.48	12.85	13.22	13.59	13.97
33	8.73	9.10	9.47	9.85	10.22	10.60	10.98	11.36	11.73	12.11	12.49	12.88	13.26	13.64	14.02	14.41
34	8.99	9.37	9.76	10.15	10.53	10.92	11.31	11.70	12.09	12.48	12.88	13.27	13.66	14.06	14.45	14.85
35	9.25	9.65	10.05	10.45	10.85	11.25	11.65	12.05	12.45	12.85	13.26	13.66	14.07	14.48	14.89	15.29
36	9.52	9.93	10.34	10.75	11.16	11.57	11.98	12.40	12.81	13.23	13.64	14.06	14.48	14.90	15.32	15.74
37	9.78	10.20	10.63	11.05	11.47	11.89	12.32	12.74	13.17	13.60	14.03	14.46	14.89	15.32	15.75	16.19
38	10.05	10.48	10.91	11.35	11.78	12.22	12.66	13.09	13.53	13.97	14.41	14.85	15.30	15.74	16.19	16.63
39	10.32	10.76	11.20	11.65	12.10	12.54	12.99	13.44	13.89	14.35	14.80	15.25	15.71	16.17	16.62	17.08
40	10.58	11.04	11.49	11.95	12.41	12.87	13.33	13.79	14.26	14.72	15.19	15.65	16.12	16.59	17.06	17.53
41	10.85	11.32	11.78	12.25	12.72	13.20	13.67	14.14	14.62	15.10	15.57	16.05	16.53	17.01	17.50	17.98
42	11.12	11.60	12.08	12.56	13.04	13.52	14.01	14.50	14.98	15.47	15.96	16.45	16.95	17.44	17.94	18.43
43	11.38	11.87	12.37	12.86	13.36	13.85	14.35	14.85	15.35	15.85	16.35	16.86	17.36	17.87	18.38	18.89
44	11.65	12.15	12.66	13.16	13.67	14.18	14.69	15.20	15.71	16.23	16.74	17.26	17.78	18.30	18.82	19.34
45	11.92	12.44	12.95	13.47	13.99	14.51	15.03	15.55	16.08	16.61	17.13	17.66	18.19	18.73	19.26	19.79
46	12.19	12.72	13.24	13.77	14.31	14.84	15.37	15.91	16.45	16.99	17.53	18.07	18.61	19.16	19.70	20.25
47	12.46	13.00	13.54	14.08	14.62	15.17	15.72	16.26	16.81	17.37	17.92	18.47	19.03	19.59	20.15	20.71
48	12.73	13.28	13.83	14.39	14.94	15.50	16.06	16.62	17.18	17.75	18.31	18.88	19.45	20.02	20.59	21.16
49	13.00	13.56	14.13	14.69	15.26	15.83	16.40	16.98	17.55	18.13	18.71	19.29	19.87	20.45	21.04	21.62
50	13.27	13.84	14.42	15.00	15.58	16.16	16.75	17.33	17.92	18.51	19.10	19.69	20.29	20.89	21.48	22.08
51	13.54	14.13	14.72	15.31	15.90	16.50	17.09	17.69	18.29	18.89	19.50	20.10	20.71	21.32	21.93	22.55
52	13.81	14.41	15.01	15.62	16.22	16.83	17.44	18.05	18.66	19.28	19.89	20.51	21.13	21.76	22.38	23.01
53	14.08	14.69	15.31	15.92	16.54	17.16	17.78	18.41	19.03	19.66	20.29	20.92	21.56	22.19	22.83	23.47
54	14.36	14.98	15.61	16.23	16.86	17.50	18.13	18.77	19.41	20.05	20.69	21.34	21.98	22.63	23.28	23.94
55	14.63	15.26	15.90	16.54	17.19	17.83	18.48	19.13	19.78	20.43	21.09	21.75	22.41	23.07	23.73	24.40
56	14.90	15.55	16.20	16.85	17.51	18.17	18.83	19.49	20.15	20.82	21.49	22.16	22.83	23.51	24.19	24.87
57	15.17	15.84	16.50	17.17	17.83	18.50	19.18	19.85	20.53	21.21	21.89	22.58	23.26	23.95	24.64	25.34
58	15.45	16.12	16.80	17.48	18.16	18.84	19.53	20.21	20.91	21.60	22.29	22.99	23.69	24.39	25.10	25.80
59	15.72	16.41	17.10	17.79	18.48	19.18	19.88	20.58	21.28	21.99	22.70	23.41	24.12	24.84	25.55	26.27
60	16.00	16.70	17.40	18.10	18.81	19.52	20.23	20.94	21.66	22.38	23.10	23.82	24.55	25.28	26.01	26.75

NUMBER OF PAYMENTS	10.00%	10.25%	10.50%	10.75%	11.00%	11.25%	11.50%	11.75%	12.00%	12.25%	12.50%	12.75%	13.00%	13.25%	13.50%	13.75%
				(FINANCE CHARGE PER $100 OF AMOUNT FINANCED)												
1	0.83	0.85	0.87	0.90	0.92	0.94	0.96	0.98	1.00	1.02	1.04	1.06	1.08	1.10	1.12	1.15
2	1.25	1.28	1.31	1.35	1.38	1.41	1.44	1.47	1.50	1.53	1.57	1.60	1.63	1.66	1.69	1.72
3	1.67	1.71	1.76	1.80	1.84	1.88	1.92	1.96	2.01	2.05	2.09	2.13	2.17	2.22	2.26	2.30
4	2.09	2.14	2.20	2.25	2.30	2.35	2.41	2.46	2.51	2.57	2.62	2.67	2.72	2.78	2.83	2.88
5	2.51	2.58	2.64	2.70	2.77	2.83	2.89	2.96	3.02	3.08	3.15	3.21	3.27	3.34	3.40	3.46
6	2.94	3.01	3.08	3.16	3.23	3.31	3.38	3.45	3.53	3.60	3.68	3.75	3.83	3.90	3.97	4.05
7	3.36	3.45	3.53	3.62	3.70	3.78	3.87	3.95	4.04	4.12	4.21	4.29	4.38	4.47	4.55	4.64
8	3.79	3.88	3.98	4.07	4.17	4.26	4.36	4.46	4.55	4.65	4.74	4.84	4.94	5.03	5.13	5.22
9	4.21	4.32	4.43	4.53	4.64	4.75	4.85	4.96	5.07	5.17	5.28	5.39	5.49	5.60	5.71	5.82
10	4.64	4.76	4.88	4.99	5.11	5.23	5.35	5.46	5.58	5.70	5.82	5.94	6.05	6.17	6.29	6.41
11	5.07	5.20	5.33	5.45	5.58	5.71	5.84	5.97	6.10	6.23	6.36	6.49	6.62	6.75	6.88	7.01
12	5.50	5.64	5.78	5.92	6.06	6.20	6.34	6.48	6.62	6.76	6.90	7.04	7.18	7.32	7.46	7.60
13	5.93	6.08	6.23	6.38	6.53	6.68	6.84	6.99	7.14	7.29	7.44	7.59	7.75	7.90	8.05	8.20
14	6.36	6.52	6.69	6.85	7.01	7.17	7.34	7.50	7.66	7.82	7.99	8.15	8.31	8.48	8.64	8.81
15	6.80	6.97	7.14	7.32	7.49	7.66	7.84	8.01	8.19	8.36	8.53	8.71	8.88	9.06	9.23	9.41
16	7.23	7.41	7.60	7.78	7.97	8.15	8.34	8.53	8.71	8.90	9.08	9.27	9.46	9.64	9.83	10.02
17	7.67	7.86	8.06	8.25	8.45	8.65	8.84	9.04	9.24	9.44	9.63	9.83	10.03	10.23	10.43	10.63
18	8.10	8.31	8.52	8.73	8.93	9.14	9.35	9.56	9.77	9.98	10.19	10.40	10.61	10.82	11.03	11.24
19	8.54	8.76	8.98	9.20	9.42	9.64	9.86	10.08	10.30	10.52	10.74	10.96	11.18	11.41	11.63	11.85
20	8.98	9.21	9.44	9.67	9.90	10.13	10.37	10.60	10.83	11.06	11.30	11.53	11.76	12.00	12.23	12.46
21	9.42	9.66	9.90	10.15	10.39	10.63	10.88	11.12	11.36	11.61	11.85	12.10	12.34	12.59	12.84	13.08
22	9.86	10.12	10.37	10.62	10.88	11.13	11.39	11.64	11.90	12.16	12.41	12.67	12.93	13.19	13.44	13.70
23	10.30	10.57	10.84	11.10	11.37	11.63	11.90	12.17	12.44	12.71	12.97	13.24	13.51	13.78	14.05	14.32
24	10.75	11.02	11.30	11.58	11.86	12.14	12.42	12.70	12.98	13.26	13.54	13.82	14.10	14.38	14.66	14.95
25	11.19	11.48	11.77	12.06	12.35	12.64	12.93	13.22	13.52	13.81	14.10	14.40	14.69	14.98	15.28	15.57
26	11.64	11.94	12.24	12.54	12.85	13.15	13.45	13.75	14.06	14.36	14.67	14.97	15.28	15.59	15.89	16.20
27	12.09	12.40	12.71	13.03	13.34	13.66	13.97	14.29	14.60	14.92	15.24	15.56	15.87	16.19	16.51	16.83
28	12.53	12.86	13.18	13.51	13.84	14.16	14.49	14.82	15.15	15.48	15.81	16.14	16.47	16.80	17.13	17.46
29	12.98	13.32	13.66	14.00	14.33	14.67	15.01	15.35	15.70	16.04	16.38	16.72	17.07	17.41	17.75	18.10
30	13.43	13.78	14.13	14.48	14.83	15.19	15.54	15.89	16.24	16.60	16.95	17.31	17.66	18.02	18.38	18.74
31	13.89	14.25	14.61	14.97	15.33	15.70	16.06	16.43	16.79	17.16	17.53	17.90	18.27	18.63	19.00	19.38
32	14.34	14.71	15.09	15.46	15.84	16.21	16.59	16.97	17.35	17.73	18.11	18.49	18.87	19.25	19.63	20.02
33	14.79	15.18	15.57	15.95	16.34	16.73	17.12	17.51	17.90	18.29	18.69	19.08	19.47	19.87	20.26	20.66
34	15.25	15.65	16.05	16.44	16.85	17.25	17.65	18.05	18.46	18.86	19.27	19.67	20.08	20.49	20.90	21.31
35	15.70	16.11	16.53	16.94	17.35	17.77	18.18	18.60	19.01	19.43	19.85	20.27	20.69	21.11	21.53	21.95
36	16.16	16.58	17.01	17.43	17.86	18.29	18.71	19.14	19.57	20.00	20.43	20.87	21.30	21.73	22.17	22.60
37	16.62	17.06	17.49	17.93	18.37	18.81	19.25	19.69	20.13	20.58	21.02	21.46	21.91	22.36	22.81	23.25
38	17.08	17.53	17.98	18.43	18.88	19.33	19.78	20.24	20.69	21.15	21.61	22.07	22.52	22.99	23.45	23.91
39	17.54	18.00	18.46	18.93	19.39	19.86	20.32	20.79	21.26	21.73	22.20	22.67	23.14	23.61	24.09	24.56
40	18.00	18.48	18.95	19.43	19.90	20.38	20.86	21.34	21.82	22.30	22.79	23.27	23.76	24.25	24.73	25.22
41	18.47	18.95	19.44	19.93	20.42	20.91	21.40	21.89	22.39	22.88	23.38	23.88	24.38	24.88	25.38	25.88
42	18.93	19.43	19.93	20.43	20.93	21.44	21.94	22.45	22.96	23.47	23.98	24.49	25.00	25.51	26.03	26.55
43	19.40	19.91	20.42	20.94	21.45	21.97	22.49	23.01	23.53	24.05	24.57	25.10	25.62	26.15	26.68	27.21
44	19.86	20.39	20.91	21.44	21.97	22.50	23.03	23.57	24.10	24.64	25.17	25.71	26.25	26.79	27.33	27.88
45	20.33	20.87	21.41	21.95	22.49	23.03	23.58	24.12	24.67	25.22	25.77	26.32	26.88	27.43	27.99	28.55
46	20.80	21.35	21.90	22.46	23.01	23.57	24.13	24.69	25.25	25.81	26.37	26.94	27.51	28.08	28.65	29.22
47	21.27	21.83	22.40	22.97	23.53	24.10	24.68	25.25	25.82	26.40	26.98	27.56	28.14	28.72	29.31	29.89
48	21.74	22.32	22.90	23.48	24.06	24.64	25.23	25.81	26.40	26.99	27.58	28.18	28.77	29.37	29.97	30.57
49	22.21	22.80	23.39	23.99	24.58	25.18	25.78	26.38	26.98	27.59	28.19	28.80	29.41	30.02	30.63	31.24
50	22.69	23.29	23.89	24.50	25.11	25.72	26.33	26.95	27.56	28.18	28.80	29.42	30.04	30.67	31.29	31.92
51	23.16	23.78	24.40	25.02	25.64	26.26	26.89	27.52	28.15	28.78	29.41	30.05	30.68	31.32	31.96	32.60
52	23.64	24.27	24.90	25.53	26.17	26.81	27.45	28.09	28.73	29.38	30.02	30.67	31.32	31.98	32.63	33.29
53	24.11	24.76	25.40	26.05	26.70	27.35	28.00	28.66	29.32	29.98	30.64	31.30	31.97	32.63	33.30	33.97
54	24.59	25.25	25.91	26.57	27.23	27.90	28.56	29.23	29.91	30.58	31.25	31.93	32.61	33.29	33.98	34.66
55	25.07	25.74	26.41	27.09	27.77	28.44	29.13	29.81	30.50	31.18	31.87	32.56	33.26	33.95	34.65	35.35
56	25.55	26.23	26.92	27.61	28.30	28.99	29.69	30.39	31.09	31.79	32.49	33.20	33.91	34.62	35.33	36.04
57	26.03	26.73	27.43	28.13	28.84	29.54	30.25	30.97	31.68	32.39	33.11	33.83	34.56	35.28	36.01	36.74
58	26.51	27.23	27.94	28.66	29.37	30.10	30.82	31.55	32.27	33.00	33.74	34.47	35.21	35.95	36.69	37.43
59	27.00	27.72	28.45	29.18	29.91	30.65	31.39	32.13	32.87	33.61	34.36	35.11	35.86	36.62	37.37	38.13
60	27.48	28.22	28.96	29.71	30.45	31.20	31.96	32.71	33.47	34.23	34.99	35.75	36.52	37.29	38.06	38.83

NUMBER OF PAYMENTS	14.00%	14.25%	14.50%	14.75%	15.00%	15.25%	15.50%	15.75%	16.00%	16.25%	16.50%	16.75%	17.00%	17.25%	17.50%	17.75%
					(FINANCE CHARGE PER $100 OF AMOUNT FINANCED)											
1	1.17	1.19	1.21	1.23	1.25	1.27	1.29	1.31	1.33	1.35	1.37	1.40	1.42	1.44	1.46	1.48
2	1.75	1.78	1.82	1.85	1.88	1.91	1.94	1.97	2.00	2.04	2.07	2.10	2.13	2.16	2.19	2.22
3	2.34	2.38	2.43	2.47	2.51	2.55	2.59	2.64	2.68	2.72	2.76	2.80	2.85	2.89	2.93	2.97
4	2.93	2.99	3.04	3.09	3.14	3.20	3.25	3.30	3.36	3.41	3.46	3.51	3.57	3.62	3.67	3.73
5	3.53	3.59	3.65	3.72	3.78	3.84	3.91	3.97	4.04	4.10	4.16	4.23	4.29	4.35	4.42	4.48
6	4.12	4.20	4.27	4.35	4.42	4.49	4.57	4.64	4.72	4.79	4.87	4.94	5.02	5.09	5.17	5.24
7	4.72	4.81	4.89	4.98	5.06	5.15	5.23	5.32	5.40	5.49	5.58	5.66	5.75	5.83	5.92	6.00
8	5.32	5.42	5.51	5.61	5.71	5.80	5.90	6.00	6.09	6.19	6.29	6.38	6.48	6.58	6.67	6.77
9	5.92	6.03	6.14	6.25	6.35	6.46	6.57	6.68	6.78	6.89	7.00	7.11	7.22	7.32	7.43	7.54
10	6.53	6.65	6.77	6.88	7.00	7.12	7.24	7.36	7.48	7.60	7.72	7.84	7.96	8.08	8.19	8.31
11	7.14	7.27	7.40	7.53	7.66	7.79	7.92	8.05	8.18	8.31	8.44	8.57	8.70	8.83	8.96	9.09
12	7.74	7.89	8.03	8.17	8.31	8.45	8.59	8.74	8.88	9.02	9.16	9.30	9.45	9.59	9.73	9.87
13	8.36	8.51	8.66	8.81	8.97	9.12	9.27	9.43	9.58	9.73	9.89	10.04	10.20	10.35	10.50	10.66
14	8.97	9.13	9.30	9.46	9.63	9.79	9.96	10.12	10.79	10.45	10.67	10.78	10.95	11.11	11.28	11.45
15	9.59	9.76	9.94	10.11	10.29	10.47	10.64	10.82	11.00	11.17	11.35	11.53	11.71	11.88	12.06	12.24
16	10.20	10.39	10.58	10.77	10.95	11.14	11.33	11.52	11.71	11.90	12.09	12.28	12.46	12.65	12.84	13.03
17	10.82	11.02	11.22	11.42	11.62	11.82	12.02	12.22	12.42	12.62	12.83	13.03	13.23	13.43	13.63	13.83
18	11.45	11.66	11.87	12.08	12.29	12.50	12.72	12.93	13.14	13.35	13.57	13.78	13.99	14.21	14.42	14.64
19	12.07	12.30	12.52	12.74	12.97	13.19	13.41	13.64	13.86	14.09	14.31	14.54	14.76	14.99	15.22	15.44
20	12.70	12.93	13.17	13.41	13.64	13.88	14.11	14.35	14.59	14.82	15.06	15.30	15.54	15.77	16.01	16.25
21	13.33	13.58	13.82	14.07	14.32	14.57	14.82	15.06	15.31	15.56	15.81	16.06	16.31	16.56	16.81	17.07
22	13.96	14.22	14.48	14.74	15.00	15.26	15.52	15.78	16.04	16.30	16.57	16.83	17.09	17.36	17.62	17.88
23	14.59	14.87	15.14	15.41	15.68	15.96	16.23	16.50	16.78	17.05	17.32	17.60	17.88	18.15	18.43	18.70
24	15.23	15.51	15.80	16.08	16.37	16.65	16.94	17.22	17.51	17.80	18.09	18.37	18.66	18.95	19.24	19.53
25	15.87	16.17	16.46	16.76	17.06	17.35	17.65	17.95	18.25	18.55	18.85	19.15	19.45	19.75	20.05	20.36
26	16.51	16.82	17.13	17.44	17.75	18.06	18.37	18.68	18.99	19.30	19.62	19.93	20.24	20.56	20.87	21.19
27	17.15	17.47	17.80	18.12	18.44	18.76	19.09	19.41	19.74	20.06	20.39	20.71	21.04	21.37	21.69	22.02
28	17.80	18.13	18.47	18.80	19.14	19.47	19.81	20.15	20.48	20.82	21.16	21.50	21.84	22.18	22.52	22.86
29	18.45	18.79	19.14	19.49	19.83	20.18	20.53	20.89	21.23	21.58	21.94	22.29	22.64	22.99	23.35	23.70
30	19.10	19.45	19.81	20.17	20.54	20.90	21.26	21.62	21.99	22.35	22.72	23.08	23.45	23.81	24.18	24.55
31	19.75	20.12	20.49	20.87	21.24	21.61	21.99	22.37	22.74	23.12	23.50	23.88	24.26	24.64	25.02	25.40
32	20.40	20.79	21.17	21.56	21.95	22.33	22.72	23.11	23.50	23.89	24.28	24.68	25.07	25.46	25.86	26.25
33	21.06	21.46	21.85	22.25	22.65	23.06	23.46	23.86	24.26	24.67	25.07	25.48	25.88	26.29	26.70	27.11
34	21.72	22.13	22.54	22.95	23.37	23.78	24.19	24.61	25.03	25.44	25.86	26.28	26.70	27.12	27.54	27.97
35	22.38	22.80	23.23	23.65	24.08	24.51	24.94	25.36	25.79	26.23	26.66	27.09	27.52	27.96	28.39	28.83
36	23.04	23.48	23.92	24.35	24.80	25.24	25.68	26.12	26.57	27.01	27.46	27.90	28.35	28.80	29.25	29.70
37	23.70	24.16	24.61	25.06	25.51	25.97	26.42	26.88	27.34	27.80	28.26	28.72	29.18	29.64	30.10	30.57
38	24.37	24.84	25.30	25.77	26.24	26.70	27.17	27.64	28.11	28.59	29.06	29.53	30.01	30.49	30.96	31.44
39	25.04	25.52	26.00	26.48	26.96	27.44	27.92	28.41	28.89	29.38	29.87	30.36	30.85	31.34	31.83	32.32
40	25.71	26.20	26.70	27.19	27.69	28.18	28.68	29.18	29.68	30.18	30.68	31.19	31.68	32.19	32.69	33.20
41	26.39	26.89	27.40	27.91	28.41	28.92	29.44	29.95	30.46	30.97	31.49	32.01	32.52	33.04	33.56	34.08
42	27.06	27.58	28.10	28.62	29.15	29.67	30.19	30.72	31.25	31.78	32.31	32.84	33.37	33.90	34.44	34.97
43	27.74	28.27	28.81	29.34	29.88	30.42	30.96	31.50	32.04	32.58	33.13	33.67	34.22	34.76	35.31	35.86
44	28.42	28.97	29.52	30.07	30.62	31.17	31.72	32.28	32.83	33.39	33.95	34.51	35.07	35.63	36.19	36.76
45	29.11	29.67	30.23	30.79	31.36	31.92	32.49	33.06	33.63	34.20	34.77	35.35	35.92	36.50	37.08	37.66
46	29.79	30.36	30.94	31.52	32.10	32.68	33.26	33.84	34.43	35.01	35.60	36.19	36.78	37.37	37.96	38.56
47	30.48	31.07	31.66	32.25	32.84	33.44	34.03	34.63	35.23	35.83	36.43	37.04	37.64	38.25	38.86	39.46
48	31.17	31.77	32.37	32.98	33.59	34.20	34.81	35.42	36.03	36.65	37.27	37.88	38.50	39.13	39.75	40.37
49	31.86	32.48	33.09	33.71	34.34	34.96	35.59	36.21	36.84	37.47	38.10	38.74	39.37	40.01	40.65	41.29
50	32.55	33.18	33.82	34.45	35.09	35.73	36.37	37.01	37.65	38.30	38.94	39.59	40.24	40.89	41.55	42.20
51	33.25	33.89	34.54	35.19	35.84	36.49	37.15	37.81	38.46	39.17	39.79	40.45	41.11	41.78	42.45	43.12
52	33.95	34.61	35.27	35.93	36.60	37.27	37.94	38.61	39.28	39.96	40.63	41.31	41.99	42.67	43.36	44.04
53	34.65	35.32	36.00	36.68	37.36	38.04	38.72	39.41	40.10	40.79	41.48	42.17	42.87	43.57	44.27	44.97
54	35.35	36.04	36.73	37.42	38.12	38.82	39.52	40.22	40.92	41.63	42.33	43.04	43.75	44.47	45.18	45.90
55	36.05	36.76	37.46	38.17	38.88	39.60	40.31	41.03	41.74	42.47	43.19	43.91	44.64	45.37	46.10	46.83
56	36.76	37.48	38.20	38.92	39.65	40.38	41.11	41.84	42.57	43.31	44.05	44.79	45.53	46.27	47.02	47.77
57	37.47	38.20	38.94	39.68	40.42	41.16	41.91	42.65	43.40	44.15	44.91	45.66	46.42	47.18	47.94	48.71
58	38.18	38.93	39.68	40.43	41.19	41.95	42.71	43.47	44.23	45.00	45.77	46.54	47.32	48.09	48.87	49.65
59	38.89	39.66	40.42	41.19	41.96	42.74	43.51	44.29	45.07	45.85	46.64	47.42	48.21	49.01	49.80	50.60
60	39.61	40.39	41.17	41.95	42.74	43.53	44.32	45.11	45.91	46.71	47.51	48.31	49.12	49.92	50.73	51.55

ANNUAL PERCENTAGE RATE

NUMBER OF PAYMENTS	18.00%	18.25%	18.50%	18.75%	19.00%	19.25%	19.50%	19.75%	20.00%	20.25%	20.50%	20.75%	21.00%	21.25%	21.50%	21.75%
					(FINANCE CHARGE PER $100 OF AMOUNT FINANCED)											
1	1.50	1.52	1.54	1.56	1.58	1.60	1.62	1.65	1.67	1.69	1.71	1.73	1.75	1.77	1.79	1.81
2	2.26	2.29	2.32	2.35	2.38	2.41	2.44	2.48	2.51	2.54	2.57	2.60	2.63	2.66	2.70	2.73
3	3.01	3.06	3.10	3.14	3.18	3.23	3.27	3.31	3.35	3.39	3.44	3.48	3.52	3.56	3.60	3.65
4	3.78	3.83	3.88	3.94	3.99	4.04	4.10	4.15	4.20	4.25	4.31	4.36	4.41	4.47	4.52	4.57
5	4.54	4.61	4.67	4.74	4.80	4.86	4.93	4.99	5.06	5.12	5.18	5.25	5.31	5.37	5.44	5.50
6	5.32	5.39	5.46	5.54	5.61	5.69	5.76	5.84	5.91	5.99	6.06	6.14	6.21	6.29	6.36	6.44
7	6.09	6.18	6.26	6.35	6.43	6.52	6.60	6.69	6.78	6.86	6.95	7.04	7.12	7.21	7.29	7.38
8	6.87	6.96	7.06	7.16	7.26	7.35	7.45	7.55	7.64	7.74	7.84	7.94	8.03	8.13	8.23	8.33
9	7.65	7.76	7.87	7.97	8.08	8.19	8.30	8.41	8.52	8.63	8.73	8.84	8.95	9.06	9.17	9.28
10	8.43	8.55	8.67	8.79	8.91	9.03	9.15	9.27	9.39	9.51	9.63	9.75	9.88	10.00	10.12	10.24
11	9.22	9.35	9.49	9.62	9.75	9.88	10.01	10.14	10.28	10.41	10.54	10.67	10.80	10.94	11.07	11.20
12	10.02	10.16	10.30	10.44	10.59	10.73	10.87	11.02	11.16	11.31	11.45	11.59	11.74	11.88	12.02	12.17
13	10.81	10.97	11.12	11.28	11.43	11.59	11.74	11.90	12.05	12.21	12.36	12.52	12.67	12.83	12.99	13.14
14	11.61	11.78	11.95	12.11	12.28	12.45	12.61	12.78	12.95	13.11	13.28	13.45	13.62	13.79	13.95	14.12
15	12.42	12.59	12.77	12.95	13.13	13.31	13.49	13.67	13.85	14.03	14.21	14.39	14.57	14.75	14.93	15.11
16	13.22	13.41	13.60	13.80	13.99	14.18	14.37	14.56	14.75	14.94	15.13	15.33	15.52	15.71	15.90	16.10
17	14.04	14.24	14.44	14.64	14.85	15.05	15.25	15.46	15.66	15.86	16.07	16.27	16.48	16.68	16.89	17.09
18	14.85	15.07	15.28	15.49	15.71	15.93	16.14	16.36	16.57	16.79	17.01	17.22	17.44	17.66	17.88	18.09
19	15.67	15.90	16.12	16.35	16.58	16.81	17.03	17.26	17.49	17.72	17.95	18.18	18.41	18.64	18.87	19.10
20	16.49	16.73	16.97	17.21	17.45	17.69	17.93	18.17	18.41	18.66	18.90	19.14	19.38	19.63	19.87	20.11
21	17.32	17.57	17.82	18.07	18.33	18.58	18.83	19.09	19.34	19.60	19.85	20.11	20.36	20.62	20.87	21.13
22	18.15	18.41	18.68	18.94	19.21	19.47	19.74	20.01	20.27	20.54	20.81	21.08	21.34	21.61	21.88	22.15
23	18.98	19.26	19.54	19.81	20.09	20.37	20.65	20.93	21.21	21.49	21.77	22.05	22.33	22.61	22.90	23.18
24	19.82	20.11	20.40	20.69	20.98	21.27	21.56	21.86	22.15	22.44	22.74	23.03	23.33	23.62	23.92	24.21
25	20.66	20.96	21.27	21.57	21.87	22.18	22.48	22.79	23.10	23.40	23.71	24.02	24.32	24.63	24.94	25.25
26	21.50	21.82	22.14	22.45	22.77	23.09	23.41	23.73	24.04	24.36	24.68	25.01	25.33	25.65	25.97	26.29
27	22.35	22.68	23.01	23.34	23.67	24.00	24.33	24.67	25.00	25.33	25.67	26.00	26.34	26.67	27.01	27.34
28	23.20	23.55	23.89	24.23	24.58	24.92	25.27	25.61	25.96	26.30	26.65	27.00	27.35	27.70	28.05	28.40
29	24.06	24.41	24.77	25.13	25.49	25.84	26.20	26.56	26.92	27.28	27.64	28.00	28.37	28.73	29.09	29.46
30	24.92	25.29	25.66	26.03	26.40	26.77	27.14	27.52	27.89	28.26	28.64	29.01	29.39	29.77	30.14	30.52
31	25.78	26.16	26.55	26.93	27.32	27.70	28.09	28.47	28.86	29.25	29.64	30.03	30.42	30.81	31.20	31.59
32	26.65	27.04	27.44	27.84	28.24	28.64	29.04	29.44	29.84	30.24	30.64	31.05	31.45	31.85	32.26	32.67
33	27.52	27.93	28.34	28.75	29.16	29.57	29.99	30.40	30.82	31.23	31.65	32.07	32.49	32.91	33.33	33.75
34	28.39	28.81	29.24	29.66	30.09	30.52	30.95	31.37	31.80	32.23	32.67	33.10	33.53	33.96	34.40	34.83
35	29.27	29.71	30.14	30.58	31.02	31.47	31.91	32.35	32.79	33.24	33.68	34.13	34.58	35.03	35.47	35.92
36	30.15	30.60	31.05	31.51	31.96	32.42	32.87	33.33	33.79	34.25	34.71	35.17	35.63	36.09	36.56	37.02
37	31.03	31.50	31.97	32.43	32.90	33.37	33.84	34.32	34.79	35.26	35.74	36.21	36.69	37.16	37.64	38.12
38	31.92	32.40	32.88	33.37	33.85	34.33	34.82	35.30	35.79	36.28	36.77	37.26	37.75	38.24	38.73	39.23
39	32.81	33.31	33.80	34.30	34.80	35.30	35.80	36.30	36.80	37.30	37.81	38.31	38.82	39.32	39.83	40.34
40	33.71	34.22	34.73	35.24	35.75	36.26	36.78	37.29	37.81	38.33	38.85	39.37	39.89	40.41	40.93	41.46
41	34.61	35.13	35.66	36.18	36.71	37.24	37.77	38.30	38.83	39.36	39.89	40.43	40.96	41.50	42.04	42.58
42	35.51	36.05	36.59	37.13	37.67	38.21	38.76	39.30	39.85	40.40	40.95	41.50	42.05	42.60	43.15	43.71
43	36.42	36.97	37.52	38.08	38.63	39.19	39.75	40.31	40.87	41.44	42.00	42.57	43.13	43.70	44.27	44.84
44	37.33	37.89	38.46	39.03	39.60	40.18	40.75	41.33	41.90	42.48	43.06	43.64	44.22	44.81	45.39	45.98
45	38.24	38.82	39.41	39.99	40.58	41.17	41.75	42.35	42.94	43.53	44.13	44.72	45.32	45.92	46.52	47.12
46	39.16	39.75	40.35	40.95	41.55	42.16	42.76	43.37	43.98	44.58	45.20	45.81	46.42	47.03	47.65	48.27
47	40.08	40.69	41.30	41.92	42.54	43.15	43.77	44.40	45.02	45.64	46.27	46.90	47.53	48.16	48.79	49.42
48	41.00	41.63	42.26	42.89	43.52	44.15	44.79	45.43	46.07	46.71	47.35	47.99	48.64	49.28	49.93	50.58
49	41.93	42.57	43.22	43.86	44.51	45.16	45.81	46.46	47.12	47.77	48.43	49.09	49.75	50.41	51.08	51.74
50	42.86	43.52	44.18	44.84	45.50	46.17	46.83	47.50	48.17	48.84	49.52	50.19	50.87	51.55	52.23	52.91
51	43.79	44.47	45.14	45.82	46.50	47.18	47.86	48.55	49.23	49.92	50.61	51.30	51.99	52.69	53.38	54.08
52	44.73	45.42	46.11	46.80	47.50	48.20	48.89	49.59	50.30	51.00	51.71	52.41	53.12	53.83	54.55	55.26
53	45.67	46.38	47.08	47.79	48.50	49.22	49.93	50.65	51.37	52.09	52.81	53.53	54.26	54.98	55.71	56.44
54	46.62	47.34	48.06	48.79	49.51	50.24	50.97	51.70	52.44	53.17	53.91	54.65	55.39	56.14	56.88	57.63
55	47.57	48.30	49.04	49.78	50.52	51.27	52.02	52.76	53.52	54.27	55.02	55.78	56.54	57.30	58.06	58.82
56	48.52	49.27	50.03	50.78	51.54	52.30	53.06	53.83	54.60	55.37	56.14	56.91	57.68	58.46	59.24	60.02
57	49.47	50.24	51.01	51.79	52.56	53.34	54.12	54.90	55.68	56.47	57.25	58.04	58.84	59.63	60.43	61.22
58	50.43	51.22	52.00	52.79	53.58	54.38	55.17	55.97	56.77	57.57	58.38	59.18	59.99	60.80	61.62	62.43
59	51.39	52.20	53.00	53.80	54.61	55.42	56.23	57.05	57.87	58.68	59.51	60.33	61.15	61.98	62.81	63.64
60	52.36	53.18	54.00	54.82	55.64	56.47	57.30	58.13	58.96	59.80	60.64	61.48	62.32	63.17	64.01	64.86

LIFE INSURANCE RATES FOR MALES (FOR FEMALES SUBTRACT 3 YEARS)*

Age	Five-year term	Age	Straight life	Age	Twenty-payment life	Age	Twenty-year endowment
20	1.85	20	5.90	20	8.28	20	13.85
21	1.85	21	6.13	21	8.61	21	14.35
22	1.85	22	6.35	22	8.91	22	14.92
23	1.85	23	6.60	23	9.23	23	15.54
24	1.85	24	6.85	24	9.56	24	16.05
25	1.85	25	7.13	25	9.91	25	17.55
26	1.85	26	7.43	26	10.29	26	17.66
27	1.86	27	7.75	27	10.70	27	18.33
28	1.86	28	8.08	28	11.12	28	19.12
29	1.87	29	8.46	29	11.58	29	20.00
30	1.87	30	8.85	30	12.05	30	20.90
31	1.87	31	9.27	31	12.57	31	21.88
32	1.88	32	9.71	32	13.10	32	22.89
33	1.95	33	10.20	33	13.67	33	23.98
34	2.08	34	10.71	34	14.28	34	25.13
35	2.23	35	11.26	35	14.92	35	26.35
36	2.44	36	11.84	36	15.60	36	27.64
37	2.67	37	12.46	37	16.30	37	28.97
38	2.95	38	13.12	38	17.04	38	30.38
39	3.24	39	13.81	39	17.81	39	31.84
40	3.52	40	14.54	40	18.61	40	33.36
41	3.79	41	15.30	41	19.44	41	34.94
42	4.04	42	16.11	42	20.31	42	36.59
43	4.26	43	16.96	43	21.21	43	38.29
44	4.50	44	17.86	44	22.15	44	40.09

*Note these tables are a sampling of age groups, premium costs, and insurance coverage that are available over 44 years of age.

NONFORFEITURE OPTIONS BASED ON $1,000 FACE VALUE

Years insurance policy in force	Straight life				Twenty-payment life				Twenty-year endowment			
	Cash value	Amount of paid-up insurance	Extended term Years	Extended term Day	Cash value	Amount of paid-up insurance	Extended term Years	Extended term Day	Cash value	Amount of paid-up insurance	Extended term Years	Extended term Day
5	29	86	9	91	71	220	19	190	92	229	23	140
10	96	259	18	76	186	521	28	195	319	520	30	160
15	148	371	20	165	317	781	32	176	610	790	35	300
20	265	550	21	300	475	1,000	Life		1,000	1,000	Life	

COMPULSORY INSURANCE (BASED ON CLASS OF DRIVER)

Bodily injury to others		Damage to someone else's property	
Class	10/20	Class	5M
10	$ 55	10	129
17	98	17	160
18	80	18	160
20	116	20	186

DAMAGE TO SOMEONE ELSE'S PROPERTY

Class	10M	25M	50M	100M
10	132	134	135	136
17	164	166	168	169
18	164	166	168	169
20	191	193	195	197

TOWING AND SUBSTITUTE TRANSPORATION

Towing and labor	$ 4
Substitute transportation	16

FIRE INSURANCE RATES PER $100 OF COVERAGE FOR BUILDINGS AND CONTENTS

Rating of area	Classification of building			
	Class A		Class B	
	Buildings	Contents	Buildings	Contents
1	.28	.35	.41	.54
2	.33	.47	.50	.60
3	.41	.50	.61	.65

FIRE INSURANCE SHORT-RATE AND CANCELLATION TABLE

Time policy in force	Percent of annual rate to be charged	Time policy in force	Percent of annual rate to be charged	Time policy in force	Percent of annual rate to be charged
Days: 5	8%	Months: 3	35	Months: 8	74
10	10	4	44	9	81
20	15	5	52	10	87
25	17	6	61	11	96
Months: 1	19	7	67	12	100
2	27				

BODILY INJURY

Class	15/30	20/40	20/50	25/50	25/60	50/100	100/300	250/500	500/1000
10	27	37	40	44	47	69	94	144	187
17	37	52	58	63	69	104	146	228	298
18	33	46	50	55	60	89	124	193	251
20	41	59	65	72	78	119	168	263	344

COLLISION

Classes	Age group	Symbols 1–3 $300 ded.	Symbol 4 $300 ded.	Symbol 5 $300 ded.	Symbol 6 $300 ded.	Symbol 7 $300 ded.	Symbol 8 $300 ded.	Symbol 10 $300 ded.
10–20	1	180	180	187	194	214	264	279
	2	160	160	166	172	190	233	246
	3	148	148	154	166	183	221	233
	4	136	136	142	160	176	208	221
	5	124	124	130	154	169	196	208

Class	Additional cost to reduce deductible	
	From $300 to $200	From $300 to $100
10	13	27
17	20	43
18	16	33
20	26	55

COMPREHENSIVE

Classes	Age group	Symbols 1–3 $300 ded.	Symbol 4 $300 ded.	Symbol 5 $300 ded.	Symbol 6 $300 ded	Symbol 7 $300 ded.	Symbol 8 $300 ded.	Symbol 10 $300 ded.
10–25	1	61	61	65	85	123	157	211
	2	55	55	58	75	108	138	185
	3	52	52	55	73	104	131	178
	4	49	49	52	70	99	124	170
	5	47	47	49	67	94	116	163

Additional cost to reduce deductible: From $300 to $200 add $4.

LOAN AMORTIZATION TABLE (MONTHLY PAYMENT PER $1,000 TO PAY PRINCIPAL AND INTEREST ON INSTALLMENT LOAN)

Terms in months	7.50%	8%	8.50%	9%	10.00%	10.50%	11.00%	11.50%	12.00%
6	$170.34	$170.58	$170.83	$171.20	$171.56	$171.81	$172.05	$172.30	$172.55
12	86.76	86.99	87.22	87.46	87.92	88.15	88.38	88.62	88.85
18	58.92	59.15	59.37	59.60	60.06	60.29	60.52	60.75	60.98
24	45.00	45.23	45.46	45.69	46.14	46.38	46.61	46.84	47.07
30	36.66	36.89	37.12	37.35	37.81	38.04	38.28	38.51	38.75
36	31.11	31.34	31.57	31.80	32.27	32.50	32.74	32.98	33.21
42	27.15	27.38	27.62	27.85	28.32	28.55	28.79	29.03	29.28
48	24.18	24.42	24.65	24.77	25.36	25.60	25.85	26.09	26.33
54	21.88	22.12	22.36	22.59	23.07	23.32	23.56	23.81	24.06
60	20.04	20.28	20.52	20.76	21.25	21.49	21.74	21.99	22.24

Terms in months	12.50%	13.00%	13.50%	14.00%	14.50%	15.00%	15.50%	16.00%
6	$172.80	$173.04	$173.29	$173.54	$173.79	$174.03	$174.28	$174.53
12	89.08	89.32	89.55	89.79	90.02	90.26	90.49	90.73
18	61.21	61.45	61.68	61.92	62.15	62.38	62.62	62.86
24	47.31	47.54	47.78	48.01	48.25	48.49	48.72	48.96
30	38.98	39.22	39.46	39.70	39.94	40.18	40.42	40.66
36	33.45	33.69	33.94	34.18	34.42	34.67	34.91	35.16
42	29.52	29.76	30.01	30.25	30.50	30.75	31.00	31.25
48	26.58	26.83	27.08	27.33	27.58	27.83	28.08	28.34
54	24.31	24.56	24.81	25.06	25.32	25.58	25.84	26.10
60	22.50	22.75	23.01	23.27	23.53	23.79	24.05	24.32

AMORTIZATION CHART (MORTGAGE PRINCIPAL AND INTEREST PER THOUSAND DOLLARS)

Term in years	$3\frac{1}{2}$%	5%	$5\frac{1}{2}$%	$6\frac{1}{2}$%	7%	$7\frac{1}{2}$%	8%	$8\frac{1}{2}$%	9%	$9\frac{1}{2}$%	10%	$10\frac{1}{2}$%	11%	$11\frac{1}{2}$%
10	9.89	10.61	10.86	11.36	11.62	11.88	12.14	12.40	12.67	12.94	13.22	13.50	13.78	14.06
12	8.52	9.25	9.51	10.02	10.29	10.56	10.83	11.11	11.39	11.67	11.96	12.25	12.54	12.84
15	7.15	7.91	8.18	8.72	8.99	9.28	9.56	9.85	10.15	10.45	10.75	11.06	11.37	11.69
17	6.52	7.29	7.56	8.12	8.40	8.69	8.99	9.29	9.59	9.90	10.22	10.54	10.86	11.19
20	5.80	6.60	6.88	7.46	7.76	8.06	8.37	8.68	9.00	9.33	9.66	9.99	10.33	10.67
22	5.44	6.20	6.51	7.13	7.44	7.75	8.07	8.39	8.72	9.05	9.39	9.73	10.08	10.43
25	5.01	5.85	6.15	6.76	7.07	7.39	7.72	8.06	8.40	8.74	9.09	9.45	9.81	10.17
30	4.50	5.37	5.68	6.33	6.66	7.00	7.34	7.69	8.05	8.41	8.78	9.15	9.53	9.91
35	3.99	5.05	5.38	6.05	6.39	6.75	7.11	7.47	7.84	8.22	8.60	8.99	9.37	9.77

Term in years	$11\frac{3}{4}$%	12%	$12\frac{1}{2}$%	$12\frac{3}{4}$%	13%	$13\frac{1}{2}$%	$13\frac{3}{4}$%	14%	$14\frac{1}{2}$%	$14\frac{3}{4}$%	15%	$15\frac{1}{2}$%
10	14.21	14.35	14.64	14.79	14.94	15.23	15.38	15.53	15.83	15.99	16.14	16.45
12	12.99	13.14	13.44	13.60	13.75	14.06	14.22	14.38	14.69	14.85	15.01	15.34
15	11.85	12.01	12.33	12.49	12.66	12.99	13.15	13.32	13.66	13.83	14.00	14.34
17	11.35	11.52	11.85	12.02	12.19	12.53	12.71	12.88	13.23	13.41	13.58	13.94
20	10.84	11.02	11.37	11.54	11.72	12.08	12.26	12.44	12.80	12.99	13.17	13.54
22	10.61	10.78	11.14	11.33	11.51	11.87	12.06	12.24	12.62	12.81	12.99	13.37
25	10.35	10.54	10.91	11.10	11.28	11.66	11.85	12.04	12.43	12.62	12.81	13.20
30	10.10	10.29	10.68	10.87	11.07	11.46	11.66	11.85	12.25	12.45	12.65	13.05
35	9.96	10.16	10.56	10.76	10.96	11.36	11.56	11.76	12.17	12.37	12.57	12.98

EXACT DAYS-IN-A-YEAR CALENDAR (EXCLUDING LEAP YEAR)

Day of month	31 Jan.	28 Feb.	31 Mar.	30 Apr.	31 May	30 June	31 July	31 Aug.	30 Sept.	31 Oct.	30 Nov.	31 Dec.
1	1	32	60	91	121	152	182	213	244	274	305	335
2	2	33	61	92	122	153	183	214	245	275	306	336
3	3	34	62	93	123	154	184	215	246	276	307	337
4	4	35	63	94	124	155	185	216	247	277	308	338
5	5	36	64	95	125	156	186	217	248	278	309	339
6	6	37	65	96	126	157	187	218	249	279	310	340
7	7	38	66	97	127	158	188	219	250	280	311	341
8	8	39	67	98	128	159	189	220	251	281	312	342
9	9	40	68	99	129	160	190	221	252	282	313	343
10	10	41	69	100	130	161	191	222	253	283	314	344
11	11	42	70	101	131	162	192	223	254	284	315	345
12	12	43	71	102	132	163	193	224	255	285	316	346
13	13	44	72	103	133	164	194	225	256	286	317	347
14	14	45	73	104	134	165	195	226	257	287	318	348
15	15	46	74	105	135	166	196	227	258	288	319	349
16	16	47	75	106	136	167	197	228	259	289	320	350
17	17	48	76	107	137	168	198	229	260	290	321	351
18	18	49	77	108	138	169	199	230	261	291	322	352
19	19	50	78	109	139	170	200	231	262	292	323	353
20	20	51	79	110	140	171	201	232	263	293	324	354
21	21	52	80	111	141	172	202	233	264	294	325	355
22	22	53	81	112	142	173	203	234	265	295	326	356
23	23	54	82	113	143	174	204	235	266	296	327	357
24	24	55	83	114	144	175	205	236	267	297	328	358
25	25	56	84	115	145	176	206	237	268	298	329	359
26	26	57	85	116	146	177	207	238	269	299	330	360
27	27	58	86	117	147	178	208	239	270	300	331	361
28	28	59	87	118	148	179	209	240	271	301	332	362
29	29	—	88	119	149	180	210	241	272	302	333	363
30	30	—	89	120	150	181	211	242	273	303	334	364
31	31	—	90	—	151	—	212	243	—	304	—	365

Note: If a leap year, add 1 day to table if February 29 falls between the two dates.